THE
ASSERTIVE
CHRISTIAN

THE ASSERTIVE CHRISTIAN

by Michael Emmons
and the Reverend David Richardson

WINSTON PRESS

Library of Congress Catalog Card Number: 80-53557
ISBN: 0-86683-755-8 (previously ISBN: 0-03-059057-4)
Printed in the United States of America

5 4 3 2

Winston Press, Inc.
430 Oak Grove
Minneapolis, Minnesota 55403

The authors and publisher gratefully acknowledge permission to reprint passages from the following works: *The Way of the Sufi* by I. Shah, copyright © 1970, E.P. Dutton & Co., Inc., New York; *All This and Snoopy Too* by C. Schulz, copyright © 1960, Fawcett Publications, Inc., New York, Wm. Ravenscroft, United Feature Syndicate, Inc.; *The Structure of Human Existence* by J.B. Cobb, Jr., copyright © MCMLXVIII, The Westminster Press, Philadelphia; *Jesus, the Son of Man* by K. Gibran, copyright © 1928, 1956, Alfred A. Knopf, New York; *Slouching Toward Bethlehem* by J.V. Didion, copyright © 1968, Farrar, Straus, & Giroux, Inc., New York; *The Gift of Inner Healing* by R.C. Stapleton, copyright © 1977, Word Books, Inc., Waco, Texas 76803; *Circulating File on Time, Space, and Patience: The Edgar Cayce Readings* by E. Cayce, copyright © 1971, The Edgar Cayce Foundation, Virginia Beach, Virginia; *How to Win Over Depression* by T. LaHaye (pp. 93-95), copyright © 1974, Zondervan Corporation, Grand Rapids, Michigan; *Assertiveness: Innovation, Application, Issues* by R.E. Alberti, ed., copyright © 1977, Impact Publishers, San Luis Obispo, California; *On Aggression* by Konrad Lorenz, copyright © 1966, Harcourt Brace Jovanovich, Inc., New York; *Guilt: Theory and Therapy* by E.V. Stein, copyright © MCMLXVIII, The Westminster Press, Philadelphia; *Women in Church and Society* by G. Harkness, copyright © 1972, Abingdon Press, Nashville. (Originally from *Familiar Letters of John and Abigail Adams* by C.F. Adams, 1898, Houghton Mifflin, Boston); "The Diary of Adam and Eve" by M. Twain, copyright © 1957, Harper & Row Publishers, Inc., New York; *You're a Winner Charlie Brown* by C. Schulz, copyright © 1966, Fawcett Publications, Inc., New York, Wm. Ravenscroft, United Feature Syndicate, Inc.; *Kerygma and Counseling* by T.C. Oden, copyright © MCMLXVI, The Westminster Press, Philadelphia; "Assertive Training and the Christian Therapist" by E.W.C. McAllister, copyright © 1975, *The Journal of Psychology and Theology*, La Miranda, California; *Your Perfect Right: A Guide to Assertive Behavior* by R. Alberti and M. Emmons, copyright © 1970, 1974, 1978, Impact Publishers, Inc., San Luis Obispo, California; *The Miracle of Dialogue* by R. Howe, copyright © 1963, Seabury Press, Inc. "All this big deal about white collar crime —" Jules Feiffer, Dist. Field Newspaper Syndicate © 1973.

ACKNOWLEDGMENTS

The creation of a book is never a solitary experience. Our dialogue began in church and in seminars as people began to question the implications of assertiveness training for Christianity. Since beginning this project, our wives, Kay Emmons and Anne Richardson, have been involved on a practical level, applying assertiveness principles to Sunday school situations and other church programs. Lenore Erickson, from the Social Science Department of Cuesta College, read the manuscript, offering valuable suggestions and questions. Her husband, Charlie, rector of St. Peter's Episcopal Church in Morro Bay, made significant contributions. Janet Barrows read the first manuscript and likewise contributed with helpful criticism.

Our thanks go to all the parishioners of Trinity United Methodist Church of Los Osos for providing the forum for the ideas presented here. Assertiveness training workshops have been conducted in many churches throughout the country, and it is evident that the Christian community welcomes these practical considerations for living.

We want to give special thanks to Sharon Stewart, whose editing made a rough manuscript readable. Thanks also to Pat Lassonde of Winston Press for the thoughtful editing at the first stages of publication.

David Richardson and Michael Emmons

TABLE OF CONTENTS

CHAPTER   Page

I.   Introduction   1
II   Assertiveness and Religious Notions of Self-Denial   17
III.   The Assertive Jesus   29
IV.   But What About Meekness?   43
V.   Anger Without Sin   57
VI.   Dealing with Aggression in Oneself and Others   67
VII.   Assertive Courage and Trust   81
VIII.   Assertiveness and the Reality of Guilt   89
IX.   Assertiveness in the Christian Community   103
X.   Out of the Shadow of Man   119
XI.   Assertiveness and the Responsible Self   133
XII.   Assertiveness Training and Christian Counseling   141

APPENDIX

I.   Assertive Training and the Christian Therapist   151
    Edward W.C. McAllister
II.   Books on Assertiveness   167

INTRODUCTION

Is there a conflict between being assertive and being religious? Is it acceptable for a person with high religious or spiritual ideals to become angry and to legitimately express that anger? How do you deal with guilt feelings in expressing or not expressing yourself? Should you love your neighbor as yourself even if you have an irresolvable conflict? Was Jesus assertive? Is outward expression of religious and spiritual values equally as important as inner expression? These and other related questions will be the focus of this book. Our purpose is to provide thoughtful philosophical discussion *and* practical guidelines for assertiveness training *within* a religious context. While we do not pretend to know all the answers, even for ourselves, we hope that this work will enable you to deal with your life more adequately.

ABOUT THE WORD "GOD"

Throughout this book we will be using the term "God" to refer to that which is ultimate. Over the centuries men and women have attested to experiences with a reality or power which is beyond them. This reality has been called many names, among them, God, Brahman, Being, Allah. Nearly all religions have recognized the limitation of such naming. In our century some have even suggested new names free from all past associations. It is not, however, our intention to argue with the theologians and philosophers about the best names; we leave name preference to the reader. We do wish to recognize, however, that transcendent power which men and women have felt in their deepest spiritual and reflective moments, and we believe that self-assertion must take into consideration not only others with whom we relate, but also this ultimate dimension to life. The name "God" is the most familiar symbol in our culture for the ultimate, and for this reason, it is the name we use.

Historically, people have described their relationship to God in different ways. Some have experienced God *within* ("immanent") as very much a part of themselves, while others have experienced God *without* or *beyond* ("transcendent"). As we encounter God who is both in and beyond us, we are led to new self-understanding and a sense of oneness with God and the world.

Individuals should be able to reach full potential both inwardly and outwardly. If you learn to focus more clearly upon true inward feelings and then are unable or unwilling to express or develop those feelings, the result will be incomplete expression as a fully functioning person. Because inner and outer development or expressions actually are manifestations of the same reality, one of these cannot be stressed over the other. Too many individuals and groups are overly concerned with developing *either* inner spiritual nature *or* the outward manifestation of that nature, forgetting that *both* need to be stressed. Our experience has convinced us that both inward and outward religious experience lead one to become more self-aware, self-assured, and assertive.

RELIGIOUS EXISTENCE AND ASSERTIVE BEHAVIOR ARE COMPLEMENTARY

We believe that many principles of religion and assertiveness training are similar. The basic premise of assertiveness training, for example, is that we are all equal on a person-to-person level. We can also state this as "Do unto others as you would have them do unto you." The basis of relationships should not be in terms of money, religion, position, race, sex, age but should be centered on treating each other fairly and honestly no matter what one's station in life happens to be.

The contemporary religious song, "They'll Know We Are Christians By Our Love," has the words, "We'll guard each man's dignity, and save each man's pride."[1] While being the essence of religious action, this is also an expression of what is essential to assertiveness training. As we will demonstrate later, even turning the other cheek can be a way of guarding each person's dignity and pride. Rather than being a non-assertive form of behavior, as it is often interpreted to be, it is one of the most assertive acts.

We do not deny, however, that many interpreters of religion focus on *repressive rather than assertive principles*. In the third edition of *Your Perfect Right*,[2] the story is told of a young woman who had fears and doubts about standing up for and feeling good about herself partly due to her religious upbringing. She could still remember from her childhood a sign hanging in the Sunday school room: The formula for *joy* is Jesus first, Others second, Yourself last. The book went on to state that, unfortunately, to many Christians such messages mean quite pointedly "don't step out ahead of others," "let others take advantage of you," "turn the other cheek," "keep your feelings inside." There seems to be a religiously-based idea among many people that they must never feel good about themselves.

This book will attempt to clarify the issues that seem to confuse many of us in our strivings to lead lives that are based upon high ideals in relationships. We will attempt to clear up some negative misinterpretations of our lives which have been fostered by religious training or beliefs and make a positive statement leading toward healthy and ethical behavior.

As a minister and a psychologist, we have witnessed inspirational and healthful assertiveness principles within religion. These principles have been all too often overlooked by many religious leaders and psychologists. We will focus on the assertive elements of religion, showing their implication for personal behavior, the church, and society.

HOW A-T BEGAN

Assertiveness training (A-T) has been in existence for at least twenty-five years. Close to twenty books have been devoted to explaining its benefits, most written since 1975.[3] Although not the originators of assertiveness training, Robert Alberti and Michael Emmons wrote the first book on the subject, *Your Perfect Right*, in 1970, with revisions in 1974 and 1978. It stated many of the basic concepts of A-T and still provides the underlying foundation for much of what is being done today. Following a short history of A-T and of religious writings within the A-T field, we will summarize its concepts.

Assertiveness training officially began in 1952, when Joseph Wolpe,[4] a psychiatrist presently at Temple University in Philadelphia, identified the therapeutic approach. In his introductory material, Wolpe referred to Andrew Salter as the "pioneer of assertive behavior" for his early contributions contained in *Conditioned Reflex Therapy*, written in 1949.[5] Salter did not use the term assertive behavior, but he discussed very similar concepts in terms of his descriptions of excitatory and inhibitory personalities. In actuality, there have been other references to this type of behavior at least as far back as 1937.

ASSERTIVENESS TRAINING AND RELIGION

Several resources in recent years dealt with the relationship between assertiveness training and religious concepts. In 1976, while a student at Saint Meinrad College, Indiana, Ethan J. Allen, Jr. wrote a senior research paper which discussed religious training and assertiveness training.[6] Allen described the "nice-guy" syndrome, observing that seminarians have a reputation for being too soft because they are characteristically cheerful in the face of insult and unassertive when others disregard their rights. He indicated that these responses lead others to regard the seminarian as a Casper Milquetoast. Priest-counselors had taken notice of these traits in their students and intended to begin offering programs to help them be more assertive, according to Allen.

Randolph Sanders, presently a doctoral student at the Graduate School of Psychology, Fuller Theological Seminary, wrote a master's thesis on assertiveness training and religion in 1976 while at Stephen F. Austin State University.[7] He combined a program of Christian religious education with roleplaying techniques in order to increase assertive behavior. A group of twenty-six college students who were low in assertiveness and had a conservative theological orientation participated in the study. Results showed that those assigned to either a religiously-oriented A-T group or a standard A-T group increased in assertive behavior. Sanders had hoped to demonstrate that the religiously-oriented group would learn assertive skills sooner than a regular A-T group.

This did not occur, but the results did show that A-T can help the religiously conservative individual develop assertive behavior.

The *Journal of Psychology and Theology* (1975), contains excellent material about the relationship between religion and assertiveness training.[8] In his article, "Assertive Training and the Christian Therapist," Edward W. C. McAllister maintains that A-T gives the Christian therapist a useful tool to help clients grow, to relieve anxiety, and to function in a meaningful way in interpersonal relationships. He believes that many Christians are in need of A-T because they view being non-assertive as part of Christianity. We have enclosed McAllister's complete paper in Appendix I, since it is a valuable contribution to a more thorough understanding of A-T within the context of religious living. At this point, it would be good for the reader to turn to Appendix I and read McAllister's work to gain a better background in A-T as such and from a religious viewpoint in particular.

In 1977 Michael Emmons gave a presentation at the American Psychological Association meeting held in San Francisco. His topic was "Resolution of Conflict Between Assertiveness and Religious Socialization Messages." He discussed turning the other cheek, meekness, and anger.

David Augsburger wrote the first book that links assertiveness and religion: *Anger and Assertiveness in Pastoral Care*.[9] Released in 1979, the book illustrates how pastors can handle anger and aggression constructively.

Michael Emmons, along with C. Markam Barry, an Atlanta psychiatrist, read a second paper on assertiveness and religion in March, 1980, at The American Personnel and Guidance Association meeting in Atlanta. The title of this session was "Assertiveness and Religion: A Successful Marriage?" Emmons and

Barry stressed that assertiveness and religion are in fact compatible. The most recent work concerning A-T and religion is the June, 1980 special issue of *Assert: A Newsletter of Assertive Behavior and Personal Development*.[10] The articles in that issue deal with issues surrounding the union of assertiveness and religion. The authors are ministers, Catholic sisters, social workers, psychologists, a psychology doctoral student in a seminary, and those who have been trained both in psychology and religion. The writers came from varying religious perspectives: Catholic, Methodist, Presbyterian, Southern Baptist. Titles of the articles are as follows: "Assertiveness and Religion," by Michael L. Emmons; "Issues in A-T with Conservative Christians," by Randolph K. Sanders; "But Isn't It Wrong for Christians to Be Assertive?" by Sisters Michelle Meyers and Kay O'Neil; "Assertiveness Training and Religious Institutions," by David Duke and Larry D. Clanton; "The Assertive Jesus," by David Richardson; "Assertive Behavior and Religion: A Compatible Duo?" by Candace E. Kiely.

THE BASICS OF ASSERTIVENESS

The following chart discusses the differences between three types of behavior: non-assertive, aggressive, and assertive behavior. Essentially, the person who reacts non-assertively holds his or her feelings inside in a given situation, but does not feel good about doing so. The person who reacts aggressively expresses those feelings, but at the expense of others and himself or herself. The chart fails to point out that aggressive behavior often results in guilt and thus is not truly self-enhancing or self-expressive. There is an optimum way to enhance and express oneself which does not involve hurting others. This alternative is depicted in the chart as assertive behavior. Assertive behavior is such that one can openly and honestly express himself or herself without running roughshod over other people.

Non-Assertive Behavior	Aggressive Behavior	Assertive Behavior
As Actor	*As Actor*	*As Actor*
Self-denying	Self-enhancing at expense of another	Self-enhancing
Inhibited	Expressive	Expressive
Hurt, anxious	Depreciates others	Feels good about self
Allows others to choose for him	Chooses for others	Chooses for self
Does not achieve desired goal	Achieves desired goal by hurting others	May achieve desired goal
As Acted Upon	*As Acted Upon*	*As Acted Upon*
Guilty or angry	Self-denying	Self-enhancing
Depreciates actor	Hurt, defensive, humiliated	Expressive
Achieves desired goal at actor's expense	Does not achieve desired goal	May achieve desired goal

---

Robert E. Alberti and Michael L. Emmons, *Your Perfect Right: A Guide to Assertive Behavior*, 3rd ed. (San Luis Obispo, Calif.: Impact Publishers, Inc., 1978). Reprinted by permission.

Whether behavior is assertive, non-assertive, or aggressive in manner is much more than a matter of words. The components of each of these include such things as visual contact, voice quality, facial expressions, hand gestures, and bodily posture. Even when the actual content is held constant, these other factors are vital. Imagine saying the words "I love you" in each of the three ways. A non-assertive "I love you" would come out as a whisper with eyes downcast, body slumping, feet shuffling. Said aggressively, "I love you" comes out with a hard stare, fist clenched, teeth gritted, voice yelling. We feel that the assertive way to say "I love you" would be to have good eye contact, that is, without having the eyes diverted or staring, a relaxed body, one that is not slumping or obviously tense, and a well-modulated voice, neither whispering nor yelling. The words we use obviously are important, but these other qualities also are essential in communicating. The following examples will further clarify differences among the three styles:

If you are shortchanged while shopping, you might react as follows:

Non-Assertive: Holding your head down, you say nothing or mumble something the clerk does not hear, not wanting to create a stir. However, you feel cheated by the store and silently vow never to return.

Aggressive: You slam the money down on the counter and in a loud, belligerent voice say, "What are you doing—trying to rip me off?" Your eye contact is rather intimidating.

Assertive: You quickly point out in a firm, clear voice, with good eye contact, that you believe you have been shortchanged and would like the clerk to recalculate the amount.

As a second example, let us say that someone has given you a great compliment about your hair. Again, you can respond in one of three ways:

Non-Assertive: You hang your head, blush, and say, "Oh gee, it's nothing special." Then you shrug your shoulders and stand there feeling awkward.

Aggressive: You hastily say, "Well, the only thing you can say about that is that you must need glasses!" Your tone is sarcastic or flippant.

Assertive: Smiling and looking directly at your complimentor, you say, "Well, thank you very much, that makes me feel good."

There are many other situations we could describe, but the basic elements of the three styles of response would remain the same. The goal of an assertiveness trainer is to help each person monitor his or her interactions in life in order to handle new situations as they arise without suppressing feelings. Punching a punching bag or having a beer may rid one of frustration caused by holding feelings inside, but the fallacy behind this type of approach is that typically the individual will react the same way the next time. Most of us cannot be continually spending our time releasing pent-up feelings. The best way to handle feelings is to express them in an open, honest, forthright manner, one that does not deny one's feelings or the feelings of others.

The question of choice usually arises in any discussion of being assertive. "Aren't there times when I will decide I do not wish to be assertive?" you may ask. The answer is a definite "yes," as long as you are making this choice knowing that you have the skills necessary to be assertive if you so desire. In other words,

there are times when it is inappropriate to be assertive.
Perhaps you decide not to tell the next-door neighbors
about their noisy dog because they smashed their car
last week and their septic tank overflowed yesterday. Or
you may not return your poorly-prepared meal at the
restaurant, because the cook is new and already under
pressure to perform by the owner and the waiters or
waitresses. Being assertive does not mean applying the
skills indiscriminately.

What we are trying to do in assertiveness training is
to teach people to analyze each interaction in their lives,
whether it be dealing with the boss or one's spouse or
one's parents or one's roommates or one's teachers and
to use the appropriate response. Perhaps it could be
learning to be assertive rather than non-assertive or
aggressive in dealing with sexual matters or money
matters. No matter what the general area of concern or
the specific situation of concern, the key principle is the
same—learning to express one's feelings appropriately—
not holding them in or releasing them aggressively.

Although it is easy to observe that not expressing
oneself is non-assertive, expressing oneself aggressively is
also a result of not handling one's feelings in an
assertive manner. By not using the safety valve of
assertion, one allows feelings to build to inappropriate
levels. Since those feelings must come out eventually,
they usually come out against the low person on one's
totem pole—oneself or others. If you are the low person
on your totem pole, your pent-up feelings may appear as
psychosomatic complaints such as headaches, stomach
aches, and rashes, or as a variety of psychological
complaints such as being indecisive, wanting to "get
away from it all," drinking too much, or eating too
much. If others are low on your totem pole, your pent-
up feelings may be expressed in direct outbursts or in
terms of excessive gossiping, hating others, racism.

That none of us is always assertive is apparent. We are non-assertive at times, aggressive at times, and assertive at times. Our contention is that to be assertive, by choice, most of the time is optimum.

HOW TO BECOME ASSERTIVE

How do we teach someone to be assertive? Even though we can make guesses about the causes of non-assertion or aggression, psychologists have found that in most instances discovering causes is unnecessary. For most of us, we need only know that we have learned to behave non-assertively or aggressively and that these behaviors can be overcome by learning to be assertive in a systematic fashion. The essential steps center around watching a facilitator model or demonstrate how to handle assertively a variety of situations and rehearsing or roleplaying the situations oneself. Following this, one is given feedback by the facilitator and other participants and may watch a video tape of the performance if available. Once these steps have been completed, one may go over certain steps again after being coached in being more assertive. A vital part of the coaching process is helping one to overcome what are called cognitive barriers to being assertive—barriers such as thinking that assertion is impolite or that others will hold grudges. The learning process in assertiveness training is very active and practice-oriented. Learning new skills and changing key attitudes can produce excellent results in a relatively short period of time.

AN EXAMPLE WITH RELIGIOUS OVERTONES

We will now illustrate assertive principles in a situation where religious ideals were hindering an individual's optimum expression of feelings.

A middle-aged man, John, who had difficulty being assertive in several areas of his life, came for counseling. Much of his problem centered around his beliefs as a devout Christian. One situation which caused him particular concern involved a debt he was not able to collect. A close friend of John's owed him a considerable amount of money and was long overdue in repaying. John had mixed feelings about collecting. He stated that all he wanted was to have some portion of the money repaid on a regular basis. At the same time, he felt that he was not being loving and patient enough. He reasoned that his friend was having trouble making ends meet. John would then feel that he should "go the extra mile" and not bother him for the money. Yet the dilemma seemed to worsen because of the recurring tension about the situation's resolution.

We might characterize John's behavior as religiously motivated non-assertion. He was holding back acting upon his inner feelings because he felt he was judging his friend's motives. John was trying to second guess his friend.

The therapist focused on helping John to *act* on his concern about when his friend would repay the debt. John was helped to analyze seriously the full meaning of his Christian duty. Several ways of assertively talking with the friend were modeled for John and he rehearsed them. John came to realize that if he approached his friend assertively, John would be treating him the way he himself would like to be treated. John understood that he had been tolerant and that he now needed to act upon his innermost feelings in an outwardly assertive manner.

The result is that John now has cleared-up feelings, more money, and most importantly, a very good friend!

RESULTS OF ASSERTIVENESS TRAINING

The results of going through a standard assertiveness

training group of sixteen to twenty hours have been studied by a number of authors, and generally speaking, show that one's self-confidence increases, one's degree of anxiety in interpersonal interactions decreases, one's aggressiveness decreases, and, of course, one's assertiveness increases. If A-T is taught to someone on an individual basis, rather than as a member of a group, complex psychological complaints may go away. There are case studies that show that homosexuality, chronic vomiting in social situations, and pedophilia (child molesting) have disappeared because individuals learned to be assertive with others significant to them, such as spouses and bosses.

No method, including A-T, is a cure-all. The potential to help people in significant ways using A-T as one tool is very real, however, When you begin taking charge of many different aspects of your life by being assertive, new doors begin to open up.

NOTES INTRODUCTION

1   Peter Scholtes, copyright 1966, 1967 by F.E.L. Church
    Publications, Ltd.

2   Robert Alberti and Michael Emmons, *Your Perfect Right: A
    Guide to Assertive Behavior* (San Luis Obispo, Calif.: Impact
    Publishers, Inc., 1978), p. 10.

3   See Appendix II

4   Joseph Wolpe, *Psychotherapy by Reciprocal Inhibition* (Stanford,
    Calif.: Stanford University Press, 1958). See Appendix I for
    other works by Wolpe.

5   Andrew Salter, *Conditioned Reflex Therapy* (New York:
    Creative Age Press, 1949).

6   Ethan J. Allen, Jr., "Repression-Sensitization and the Effect of
    Assertion on Anxiety" (Senior Research Paper, Saint Meinrad
    College, Indiana, May, 1976).

7   Randolph Sanders, "The Effectiveness of a Theologically
    Oriented Approach to Assertive Training for Refusal
    Behaviors" (Master's Thesis, S.F. Austin State University,
    1976), Masters Abstracts, 14, 1976, 252 University Microfilms
    No. 13-08786.

8   Edward W.C. McAllister, "Assertive Training and the
    Christian Therapist," *Journal of Psychology and Theology*,
    Winter, 1975, pp. 19-24.

9   David Augsburger, *Anger and Assertiveness in Pastoral Care*
    (Philadelphia: Fortress Press, 1979).

10 Michael Emmons, ed., *Assert: A Newsletter of Assertive
    Behavior and Personal Development* (P.O. Box 1094, San Luis
    Obispo, Calif.).

ASSERTIVENESS AND RELIGIOUS NOTIONS OF SELF-DENIAL

It may seem at first glance that the traditional religious focus on denial of the self is in confict with assertion of the self. Pride and self-interest often have been viewed as the root of sin. The *Theologica Germanica* says, "Nothing burneth in hell except self-will." Jesus said, "If any man come after me let him deny himself." The Hindu classic, the *Bhagavad Gita*, states that those who work selfishly for results are miserable. In calm self-surrender one is freed from bondage in this life and reaches enlightenment. Buddha in the *Vinaya Pitaka* is said to teach annihilation of the self. However, close examination of the lives of the great religious figures in history show that, in spite of vigorous self-denial, these persons were highly assertive individuals. They knew themselves, their beliefs, their goals, and they also knew how to express themselves clearly.

As we shall see, self-denial for Jesus, the Buddha, Luther, Gandhi, St. Francis was the discipline needed to fulfill themselves, but it did not eliminate assertiveness.

Some authors feel that self-denial and assertion are

mutually exclusive. Ravi Ravindra holds such a perspective. His criticism of psychotherapy is that it moves in an entirely different direction from that of religion. It is concerned with the "proper functioning and self-fulfillment of a person . . . whereas spiritual schools aim at a radical reorientation and a yoking of the whole individual to a transcendent purpose."[1] He believes that psychotherapy sees the self alone as the doer while religion sees the self as an instrument of the higher will. Thus, self-realization, and we might add self-assertion, becomes "myself-realization" and "myself-assertion" rather than "God-realization" or the assertion of God's will. Accordingly, the struggle between these two perspectives is the struggle between the flesh and the Spirit.[2]

We believe that Ravindra has oversimplified the distinction between psychotherapy and religion. The definition of the self as alone or as an instrument of a higher will or reality is not excluded by all psychotherapists any more than it is clear that all schools of religion identify the self as an expression of a higher will. Certainly existential psychotherapists such as Viktor Frankl, Rollo May, Abraham Maslow, and Carl Rogers view the self in terms that are quite consistent with Western and Eastern religious traditions. The "Epigenetic Principle"[3] espoused by Neo-Freudian Erik Erikson shows a ground plan essential to the development of a person which is not at all incompatible with religious notions of the plan of God for our lives. In fact, pastoral counselors have made good use of many of the ideas of these psychologists and others to better understand the working of God.

KNOWING AND DOING: THE ESSENCE OF ASSERTION IN RELIGION

Religious and secular persons must know how to be

what they are, how to actualize the self and be assertive.
The therapy or technique for learning this should not
define the self for the student. This is the individual's
decision. "For what person knows a man's thoughts
except the spirit of the man which is in him?"
(I Corinthians 2:11).

When one is blocked in being able to assert the self,
anxiety and frustration develop. Religious circles have
long understood the crippling nature of these maladies.
The Book of James sees the cause of wars, fighting,
envy, and covetousness as the result of not being able to
obtain what one wants. "You do not have, because you
do not ask. You ask and do not receive because you ask
wrongly" (James 4:1-3).

Jesus taught his followers to actively "ask, and it
will be given you; seek, and you will find; knock, and
the door will be opened" (Matthew 7:7). Faith is not just
a static belief about X number of things; it is action
about those beliefs. Faith is the embodiment of what we
believe. This same polarity between belief and action is
found in psychotherapeutic schools—between those that
stress *knowing* and those that stress *doing*. Assertion
therapy emphasizes *doing* but not at the expense of
knowing or *insight* into the self.

This emphasis on *doing* is much more in keeping
with Western religious teachings than with Eastern
traditions. In the Judeo-Christian tradition, as well as in
Islam, it is the doing of God's will, not just knowing it,
that is important. Religion is not simply contemplative.
Self-knowledge comes to a person in action. We learn
about ourselves in our behavior. In his intellectual
autobiography, Paul Tillich describes the necessity of
both the contemplative and active side of life but
concludes that religious truth is existential truth; it
cannot be separated from practice.[4]

Assertiveness therapy is that which focuses on
practice or behavior. This focus does not lose touch

with the self in all its relationships. By a combination of internal dialogue and external expressions in behavior, one is best able to experience life at its fullest. Socrates' dictum to "know the self" is very important because misdirected assertiveness can be very destructive. Self-knowledge, however, comes in action as well as in contemplation.

EXAMPLES OF ASSERTIVENESS IN THE WORLD'S RELIGIONS

The most assertive thrust of Jesus was his ability to love, to perceive clearly and to act on those perceptions for the good of all. Herein was the contagious part of his mission, the part that had the greatest impact on others. When Christians translated this love to the social order it was demonstrated as "justice."

Jesus was greatly misunderstood, but he would not allow the confusion of his followers to change his direction. The greatest misunderstanding of his power by others was in seeing it as political power rather than love power. The rock musical *Jesus Christ Superstar* captured this dramatically when his followers sang in a frenzy about all Jesus' worldly accomplishments, concluding "You'll get the power and the glory." With a sudden hushing of the crowd, he said painfully, "Neither you, Simon, nor the fifty thousand, nor the Romans, nor the Jews, nor Judas, nor the twelve . . . understand what power is."[5]

In our century few religious leaders have understood the assertive power of love better than Martin Luther King, Jr. Shortly before his murder, he argued with Black Power advocates that a shift from non-violent tactics to violence or aggression would be self-destructive to the cause of justice and ethnic self-determination. He understood the power of love expressed in non-violence; it was the sword that "cuts without wounding."[6] Violence only multiplies violence; only love can drive out hate. According to King, black people must love white people while asserting their own rights, even though such behavior might result in beatings or persecution.

Religious leaders have long recognized love as a positive, active force. Non-assertive persons have great difficulty in expressing love or in being loved. In his great essay on love, Erich Fromm, though a critic of religion, recognizes the traditional religious idea that the one indispensable attitude necessary for the practice of the art of love is activity.[7]

We often fail to see the assertive dimensions of great religious leaders because we are focusing on the wrong things in their lives. For instance, Jesus' edict to turn the other cheek might be labeled as passive or non-assertive. Yet within the broader context of his ministry, we can see that this was the assertive thing to do in the name of love. To retreat would be cowardly and non-assertive. To turn the other cheek was a means of "hanging in there," staying with the person who behaved aggressively. It was Jesus' way of being himself and choosing his own behavior according to his values rather than simply responding to the usual dictates of aggression—"flight or fight."

In turning the other cheek one is not defeated, and one does not violate the values of the self or the values of God. In Jesus' teachings these ought to be synonymous. We must focus on what the religious teacher is trying to do rather than on what he is not doing. Non-action in one area does not mean non-assertion, for the direction may well be on another level or focus.

In Chinese religious thinking there is a great deal of discussion of the two ways of life, the *yu wei* and the *wu wei*. The first is the active way, the way of man emphasized in Confucianism; and the second, the passive way, is the way of non-action emphasized by Taoism and Ch'an Buddhism. Confucius believed that it was as necessary to know when not to act as it was to know when and how to act. He was critical, however, of the unwavering conclusions of Lao-tzu and the Taoists that passivity and non-assertion, *wu wei*, was the only course to take. He believed that there must be balance between these two. The maintenance of this balance between these polarities became the task of the Chinese religion, which is perhaps best symbolized by the Yin and the Yang.

SELF-DENIAL: ASSERTIVE OR NON-ASSERTIVE?

Non-action and self-denial in religious experience has, first of all, meant discipline so that one ultimately gains self-mastery. In popular religion this has often been misunderstood to mean self-effacement. Many religious people prize a rather morbid preoccupation with degrading oneself and denying one's own value. This is accompanied by the feeling of being "not OK," as Thomas Harris puts it.[8]

In the case of some Eastern religions, self-effacement to the point of extreme asceticism and even self-mutilation is a result of the doctrine of *no self* or *anatta*. In other words, belief that the self is entirely illusional leads some religious thinkers into radical approaches to self-denial directed toward non-being or nothingness rather than toward fulfillment. Assertive behavior from this religious perspective would simply be an exercise in futility and an extension of the illusion.

Ironically, while this doctrine of *no self* in the Eastern religious tradition leads to non-assertion and non-action, in the Western perspective ideas of *no self* have led to radical calls for action. Existentialists such as Sartre, believing that existence precedes essence, advocate that persons literally create themselves. One is nothing apart from one's decisions and actions.[9] Psychologists such as B.F. Skinner, who also argue against the essential reality of the self, have laid the psychological foundation of modern behaviorism, with emphasis on action as the only definitive reality to selfhood.[10]

Among certain Eastern religious traditions, the doctrine of *no self* leads to non-assertion and non-action because of the accompanying notion that the world of human experience is *maya*, illusion. In the West, the *no self* doctrine has been directed to the question of essence, but it has led to action because existence is seen as real rather than illusional. Human beings are what they make of themselves.

For the most part, however, self-denial and non-action have not been synonymous with non-assertion. Self-denial has been a form of self-discipline arising from the awareness that we often fool ourselves. Our perceptions of self are not congruent with who we really are. We do not easily know our own wants and needs. Worldly pursuits and possessions often take us away from the self and we become lost. To put it in Jesus' words, "What does a man gain by winning the whole world at the cost of his true self?" (Mark 8:36, N.E.B.*).

Discipline is the gain of mastery or self-control; it is not self-denigration. Christianity has been extremely uncomfortable with those who have mortified the body or chosen the path of extreme asceticism. The Christian gospel enhances the value of the person. In God's eyes we are good; we are something of value. That we are sinners is only a description of our own limitations, our fallenness, not a "put down." God so loved us that he gave his only Son. We should love ourselves as we do

*From *The New English Bible*. Copyright © 1961, 1970. The delegates of the Oxford University Press and the Syndics of the Cambridge University Press. Reprinted by permission.

our neighbor. Humility is seeing oneself in proper perspective with the world. It is not self-condemnation or self-denigration.

Through self-denial or discipline the real self is *enabled*; it finally breaks through the anxieties, ideas of inferiority, self-fulfilling prophecies, and bad feelings. It breaks through all limitations of freedom to be what it chooses. Sufi mystic Hujwiri describes the phenomenon:

> Choosing is emptying of the heart of all things other than the search for completion. This resembles a visualization that the body is empty and that all thoughts have left it for a moment, during which time the true thoughts flood in.[11]

Emptying the mind of all hindrances to the real self or inner source is essential in meditation. In Zen Buddhism this is the achievement of *no mind* or *no thought*. The *koans*, seemingly ridiculous questions, are major teaching devices in the quest for instantaneous unprecedented answers. They break the mind out of habitual structures of logic and the true self is able to flourish.

Many Buddhists are not satisfied with Gautama the Buddha's doctrine of *anatta*. According to D.T. Suzuki, "Everything without tells the individual that he is nothing, while everything within persuades him that he is everything."[12] As one sits quietly looking inward, one discovers the self.

For most of the world's religions, this discovery comes only through the denial of the illusional self, the false ego. Discipline becomes an essential component to this discovery, which in turn finally leads to true self-assertion. It is the natural way to be. Suzuki states that the true self will assert itself in one way or another. If such assertion is not natural, it will break all barriers, sometimes violently and other times pathogenically. Either way the real self is hopelessly damaged.[13]

It is precisely at this point that we see the convergence of religious interests with those of the psychologists—in particular the assertiveness trainer. Both religion and psychology recognize the need to gain mastery over the self, to intentionally decide the course of one's actions rather than to be victimized by pathogenic expressions of the self. Both religion and psychology provide a discipline for asserting oneself in a creative, healthful fashion. Gautama the Buddha, often recognized as the first great psychologist, said centuries ago, "If one man conquer in battle a thousand times a thousand men, and if another conquer himself, he is the greatest of the conquerors."[14]

NOTES CHAPTER II

1   Ravi Ravindra, "Self-Surrender: The Core of Spiritual Life," *Studies in Religion/Sciences Religieuses*, III (1973/74), p. 360.

2   Ibid., p. 359.

3   According to Erikson, "Anything that grows has a ground plan, and that out of this ground plan the parts arise, each having its time of special ascendancy, until all parts have arisen to form a functioning whole." Erik Erikson, "Identity and the Life Cycle," *Psychological Issues*, Vol. I, No. 1 (1959), p. 52.

4   Paul Tillich, *On the Boundary* (New York: Charles Scribner's Sons, 1966), p. 31.

5   Andrew Lloyd Weber and Tim Rice, *Jesus Christ Superstar*, copyright 1969 by Leeds Music, Ltd., London, England.

6   Martin Luther King, Jr., *Why We Can't Wait* (New York: Signet Books, 1963), p. 26.

7   Erich Fromm, *The Art of Loving* (New York: Bantam Books, 1963), p. 107.

8   See Thomas Harris, *I'm OK—You're OK* (New York: Harper and Row, 1967).

9   See Jean Paul Sartre, *Being and Nothingness*, trans. Hazel E. Barnes (New York: Philosophical Library, 1956).

10   See B.F. Skinner, *Beyond Freedom and Dignity* (New York: Alfred A. Knopf, 1971).

11   Quoted in Idries Shah, *The Way of the Sufi* (New York: E.P. Dutton and Company, Inc., 1970), p. 240.

12   D.T. Suzuki, "The Concept of the Self in Zen Buddhism," *Self Society and the Search for Transcendence*, ed. William Bruening (Palo Alto, Calif.: National Press Books, 1974), p. 415.

13   Ibid., p. 416.

14 From the "Dhammapada" in *The Teachings of the Compassionate Buddha*, ed. E. A. Brutt (New York: Mentor Books, 1955), p. 58.

THE ASSERTIVE JESUS

As a loving being, Jesus focused his concern by assertion of the self. Nothing, not even the threat of death, could prevent him from being and doing what he felt was the call of God upon his life. His ethics, his entire way of life, were grounded in his belief that we must be obedient to God. Each one of us has the choice to obey God or to go a different way. The way of obedience is the way of love and justice.

The assertive Jesus is seen most clearly in how he intentionally acted out the way of obedience before his disciples and those who witnessed his teaching. In a very caring way, he walked among the downtrodden and outcasts of society, eating and drinking with them. His opponents sought to shame him for this and at times charged him with violations of the law or with being an instrument of the devil for his behavior (see Matthew 12:1-14 and Matthew 12:22-24). In answer, Jesus spoke of a higher law which was more important than the legalistic prescriptions for behavior to which his critics clung. This law was the inner law of God that is written on the heart. Years before, the prophet Jeremiah had distinguished between the laws written on stone and the ultimate law of God within the hearts of men (Jeremiah 31).

Jesus believed that we must be true to this law of God, which is consistent with being true to ourselves. It is the fulfillment of all written laws. All behavior is measured by correspondence to the law of God; if the behavior is obedient, it is full of light and life-giving; if it is disobedient, it leads to darkness and death. While Jesus was assertive in his life, it was the direction of the assertion rather than assertion itself that was good. For us, the personal will can be unruly and assert itself in ways that do not correspond with God's will. We must choose the direction of our life, but to be healthful and fulfilling, this direction must correspond to God's will.

THE CALL TO BE ASSERTIVE

Jesus had an ability to call people out of non-assertive behavior to new ways of self-assertion. At the Sheep Gate Pool he met a man who had been paralyzed for thirty-eight years. Jesus saw to the heart of the matter immediately. Not commiserating or saying "Oh poor you, see how bad you've got it," Jesus said, "Do you want to be healed?" The man answered in a typically non-assertive way, "Sir, I have no man to put me into the pool when the water is troubled, and while I am going another steps down before me" (John 5:7).

The man was waiting for the magical powers of the bubbling pool to heal him. Even more important, he was waiting for someone else to carry him there rather than going to his own powerful pool of inner resource for healing. Jesus minced no words: "Rise, take up your pallet and walk" (John 5:8).

There is a similar healing story in Acts. Peter and John encountered a crippled man begging for alms at the Beautiful Gate. They gazed at him directly and Peter said, "Look at us . . . I have no silver and gold, but I give you what I have; in the name of Jesus Christ of Nazareth, walk" (Acts 3:4-6).

Charles Schulz created a delightful *Peanuts* sequence that is a healing scene. Lucy has the children and even Snoopy lie down on the ground and cough. She then stomps up and down in front of them saying, "Most germs are able to build up a defense against the various drugs used on them. That's what makes my system so good. No germ has ever been able to build up a defense against being stepped on."[1] The insight of the cartoon is that healing has to overcome resistance. It is not, however, the resistance of germs to drugs as much as the resistance of the sick person to being well that often prevents healing.

In the healing stories of the New Testament, failure to sympathize with symptoms and commiserate with the ill effectively stomps resistance. Jesus was not interested in excuses for illness; he was interested in the process that makes a person well, that makes one whole. It is no accident that the words *health*, *wholeness*, and *holy* come from the same Anglo-Saxon root word. These three dimensions work together; Jesus knew that people must give up the non-assertive, excuse-making way of life that leads to sickness.

"It is your faith that made you well" is the understanding of the healing experience that Jesus conveyed to those he touched. It was "their faith," something *within* that enabled it to happen. Faith is active; it is a decision; it is assertive. Too often faith is confused with *belief*, as though it were objects or content held to be true by the individual. Faith is not a noun even though it is used as such grammatically. It is a verb, something we do. It brings health, wholeness, and holiness.

There are other ways in which Jesus helped persons to assert themselves besides healing. Probably the most powerful was his expression of love, which Paul came later to call *grace*. Love is a therapeutic device; it is what Carl Rogers has identified as the most essential

ingredient to the therapeutic setting. He calls it
unconditional positive regard.

The story of Zacchaeus illustrates the dramatic way
Jesus could draw people out of non-assertive and isolated
behavior patterns. By lovingly demanding the best of
Zacchaeus, demanding that he be a host rather than an
outcast and a cheat, Jesus exacted a remarkable change
in the man.

When Jesus entered Jericho the streets were lined
with people (Luke 19:1-10). Zacchaeus, the chief tax
collector of the town, as disliked as he was rich, wanted
to see him. Zacchaeus was a short man and could not
see over the shoulders of the crowd. So he ran ahead
frantically and climbed a sycamore tree to see Jesus pass
by.

The story, like so many in Jesus' life, shows how
remarkably sensitive he was. He often singled out a
person in a crowd. He could relate lovingly and
personally to individuals. He told Zacchaeus to come
down. "I must stay at your house." The crowd
murmured about it, for they disliked Zacchaeus and
knew him to be a sinner. Such displeasure did not deter
Jesus from assertively showing his love and acceptance of
Zacchaeus.

Zacchaeus is typical of many of us. We all know
what it means to be isolated and lonely, and for some
people like Zacchaeus it becomes a way of life. Lonely
people sometimes build barriers for themselves which
keep them desperately in one place. They may feel the
need for relationship deeply, and yet the fear of
rejection or of asking for relationship keeps them from
assertively stepping forward. In order to protect their
feelings they put on an air of indifference, pretending
that relationship (or the lack of it) is not very
important. This gives the impression of distance.

Zacchaeus was isolated. His problem was that of
vocation. He had chosen a job which was hated by the

people, for he collected taxes for the oppressors, the
Romans. He was set outside the circle of society by his
job. Chances are he was also locked into some other
psychological cycles of isolation such as self-pity or
superiority. But Jesus looked at him and called out,
saying in effect, "I want in, I want to come and stay
with you."

Edwin Markham summarized the situation
beautifully in his poem "Outwitted":

> He drew a circle that shut me out
> Heretic, rebel, a thing to flout,
> But love and I had a wit to win
> We drew a circle that took him in![2]

Lonely people like Zacchaeus draw a circle too small to
let people in. By their own non-assertive life-styles they
have drawn the perimeters of their lives, making it very
difficult for others to reach them. Jesus, in his love,
drew a circle that was larger and that included
Zacchaeus. That was enough to get Zacchaeus to open
up and let Jesus in.

Zacchaeus was literally caught "up a tree." He was
in a terrible situation with nowhere to go. He had
always been at a distance in his relationships with
people. Rather than attempt a face-to-face encounter
with Jesus, whom he wanted to see so badly, Zacchaeus
found himself looking down at him from a tree. His was
a spectator relationship with Jesus, and one cannot be
just an observer if one wants to have personal
relationships. Jesus called the little man down. He
showed acceptance; he included him; and a dramatic
change occurred in Zacchaeus.

As with the active therapy of Alcoholics
Anonymous, which stresses *restitution* as one of its steps,
Zacchaeus gave half his goods to the poor and promised
to restore fourfold wherever he had committed fraud.

Zacchaeus was reaching out, redrawing his circle. Jesus' comment was, "Today salvation has come to this house."

AGGRESSION AND VIOLENCE TRANSFORMED

Another important dimension of Jesus' ministry was to direct people away from aggression and violence to the ways of peace. This is clearly seen in his rejection of zealotism, whose members wanted to establish the Kingdom by the sword. Oscar Cullmann even suggests that Jesus was so thorough in his denunciation of violence that he had trouble accepting the title *Messiah*, which had become identified with the zealots and the military establishment of David's Kingdom.[3]

One of Jesus' disciples, Simon, had been a zealot. This may have been Peter. According to Cullmann, Peter's name *bar Jona* is usually translated "son of Jonah," but in an old Hebrew lexicon *barjona* is a word borrowed from Akkadian, meaning "terrorist." Jesus worked with his disciples to control their aggressive ways. According to gospel accounts, he had his work cut out for him. Peter was a quick-tempered individual who at one time took up the sword to defend Jesus (John 18:10). He was rebuked by Jesus. Thus: "Put your sword back into its place; for all who take the sword will perish by the sword" (Matthew 26:52).

Two of his disciples, the sons of Zebedee, James and John, were enraged when the Samaritans refused to receive Jesus. They wanted fire called down from heaven to destroy them. Jesus rebuked them also (Luke 9:53-56).

Jesus understood that violence leads to more violence and that this cycle must be ended. *Lex taliones* "an eye for an eye" was good in the past, but now turning the other cheek should be the order. "Blessed are the peacemakers" (Matthew 5:9). He called people to settle their differences and solve their problems but not by striking out in violent ways. Anger must be dealt with as it arises and not be left to smolder. Jesus said, "So if you are offering your gift at the altar, and there remember that your brother has something against you, leave your gift there before the altar and go; first be reconciled to your brother, and then come and offer your gift" (Matthew 5:23-24).

There was no pietistic denial of anger in the way Jesus loved. He was often angry and able to express it clearly. The lines are clear between Jesus' assertive anger and his aggressive anger. For Jesus there was moral indignation about the legalism of his opponents which put law before love. They valued Sabbath Laws more highly than they did healing. They looked for easy righteousness and rejected others. At certain times, however, Jesus expressed his anger in quite aggressive ways. He was not above name calling when he was angry: "You hypocrites," "You brood of vipers," "You fools." One can speculate about what he had called the Pharisees to warrant their defense, "We were not born of fornication" (John 8:41).

Jesus was single-minded about his intention to act in accordance with what he understood to be the will of his Father. Nothing could stop his ministry. In the days preceding his entry into Jerusalem, friends warned him of the danger of continuing his work. On one occasion, a Pharisee warned him in the form of a threat, "Get away from here, for Herod wants to kill you" (Luke 13:31). He did not hesitate to answer, "Go tell that fox, 'Behold I cast out demons and perform cures today and tomorrow, and the third day I finish my course' " (Luke 13:32-33). Certainly the intention of this passage is in anticipation of the resurrection, but it also has very strong assertive connotations. He is saying, in other words, "I am going to continue until I decide my work is completed; I will not be diverted by my opponents."

JESUS WAS AGGRESSIVE

There are a few biblical records showing that Jesus was aggressive on occasion. These relate clear examples of his humanness, for a person cannot always control anger by checking to be sure that it is assertively rather than aggressively expressed. Perhaps no story has been more quoted as an example of aggressiveness than Jesus' act of cleansing the temple. He overturned the tables of the moneychangers and venders. According to Mark's account, he scolded them saying, "Is it not written, 'My house shall be called a house of prayer for all the nations?' But you have made it a den of robbers" (Mark 11:17).

That Jesus did much more than overturn the tables, chase some animals, and verbally berate the moneychangers is questionable. A whip is mentioned only in John and is clearly Messianic, establishing Jesus in the Jewish tradition of the Messiah as one who would bear the lash for the chastisement of evildoers. The whip is an emblem of authority.

Some interpreters of the passage have viewed it as Jesus' sanction for violence and the Just War. This is a misinterpretation of the message and fails to see it against the backdrop of Jesus' whole ministry, which had a singular goal, the sharing of God's love and the establishment of peace on earth. At the most, the incident can only be thought of as one moment when anger overstepped the boundary of assertive expression and aggressively exploded.

At the end of the narrative as John describes it, Jesus said, "Zeal for thy house will consume me" (John 2:17). This was a direct quote from Psalm 69 and a foreshadowing of his death at the hands of the Jews for his actions. However, one wonders if there was not a double meaning to the statement, almost a reprimand to himself for losing control.

So far we have analyzed Jesus' assertive behavior in terms of his own self-understanding as one obedient to God. This obedience was expressed in love of God and love of neighbor. This love is life-giving and it is the saving experience. Love empowered his hearers to move away from non-assertive and aggressive ways that were ineffective or destructive. We need to analyze what is implicit in Jesus' words concerning the reality of the self, or spirit. We cannot comprehend what we mean by the *assertive self* unless we are clear about the nature of the self that is being asserted. In Jesus' understanding, our self is given to us by God and we can only be truly assertive when we are what God requires of us.

The Jewish understanding of the self, spelled out in the Old Testament, is that life comes from God. It comes as *spirit* which, like the wind, is inhaled by one until death. Another metaphor for describing the self is *heart*. This is, as Rolf Knierim has said, the center of the senses, as well as the center of the will and the intellect. To have heart is to have a conscience. To have heart does not mean being merely alive; it means being spiritually disposed.[4]

Another metaphor for self is *wisdom*. It is spirit and heart at work for wholeness. Wisdom knows the heart and the world, and, if lost, one becomes a fool and dies (see Nabal, I Samuel 25).

Jesus saw self-assertion from this context. It should not lose touch with either the heart or worldly behavior. To be oneself and to be assertive demands disciplined coordination between these two dimensions of life. Jesus was therefore very critical of those who did not practice what they preached. "Woe to these hypocrites," "Woe to the blind guides." He minced no words in condemnation of this division of the self, for the tragedy of their lives was the split between what they valued and what they actualized. True righteousness is a matter of the heart, not just of outward behavior. "Woe to you, scribes and Pharisees, hypocrites! for you cleanse the outside of the cup and of the plate, but inside they are full of extortion and rapacity. You blind Pharisees! first cleanse the inside of the cup and of the plate, that the outside may also be clean" (Matthew 23:25-26).

Behavior which is out of touch with the inner self is hypocrisy; for this reason, Jesus' ministry was woven around bursts of activity and frequent retreats for reflection and prayer. The wilderness temptation story and the Garden of Gethsemane narrative are important insights into the introspective Jesus' struggles to understand himself and his motives as well as the ways in which his calling would be expressed in ministry.

Self-discipline is required to match the inner self with outward behavior. There are so many pursuits of the world that pull us away from our real selves—possessions, wealth, and even demands that everyday life makes upon us. Renunciation of these pursuits is essential. We become possessed by our possessions until we are no longer master over them or ourselves. To be assertive in the life of the spirit is to regain ourself or our spirit and put it back in control.

This is the paradox of renunciation: that giving up one's selfish pursuits leads us to the discovery of the real self. "If any man would come after me, let him deny himself . . . whoever would save his life will lose it, and whoever loses his life for my sake will find it" (Matthew 16:24-25). Jesus reiterated the familiar theme of world religions, that man has identified himself with wrong things. By giving up the false self, the true self is found.

The demands and pressures of life take us away from the most important calling in our life. When he called his disciples one answered, "Let me first go and bury my father." Jesus, who often used hyperbole for emphasis, answered him, "Leave the dead to bury their own dead" (Luke 9:59-60). Obviously, Jesus was not

advocating that corpses be left unburied. The literal
interpretation of such a passage destroys its meaning.
The point is that the concerns of life, even under the
most worthy of guises, take us away from what we ought
to pursue. They take us away from self and God.

Critics of Jesus have said that his demands were too
high, his ethic impossible for us to emulate. He had the
vision of what was possible, even if in practice we may
never achieve it. The ideal, however, serves as a
dynamic force or beckoning to his followers. Reinhold
Niebuhr has called the ethic of Jesus "the Impossible
Possibility," which we might reject out of frustration or
which might always stand before us as an upward and
onward call to actualization.[5] The Apostle Paul seems to
understand this too when he says,

> Not that I have already obtained this or am already
> perfect, but I press on to make it my own because
> Christ Jesus has made me his own. Brethren, I do
> not consider that I have made it on my own, but
> one thing I do, forgetting what lies behind and
> straining forward to what lies ahead, I press on
> toward the goal for the prize of the upward call of
> God in Christ Jesus (Philippians 3:12-14).

Actualization of the self is seen in terms of
disciplined striving to obey God. To give up is to lose
the self; it is to be satisfied with what is less than
possible for us. The demand for perfection is a demand
for the assertive self as self, which is understood as being
given to us by God.

John Knox suggests that the uniqueness of Jesus'
ethic is its very demand for perfection. Jesus asked us to
be perfect. He never diluted the demands for
righteousness or adjusted them to our moral capacities.
His ethic does not break down moral absolutes to
practical decisions. We would not expect it to do

otherwise.[6] The timelessness of his ethic is found in the fact that for every age and every person the absolute comes to us calling for a decision requiring translation into our own context. The reality is that no one is perfect but God alone (Mark 10:18). Self-righteousness is effectively shut off, but the *pursuit* of righteousness and perfection, paradoxically, are necessary for self-fulfillment and the achievement of the full life.

Jesus' teachings focus on the doing of ethics, the actualization of life, the assertion of the self. Static achievements are insignificant. Life is a process of action. The self is real, but it is in a constant state of becoming. The tragedy of life is that much is possible, but many will not actively strive for it. They will not be true to what has been given to them. "Nor do men light a lamp and put it under a bushel. . . . Let your light shine before men, that they may see your good works and give glory to your Father who is in heaven" (Matthew 5:15-16).

Jesus' assertive thrust was to be as concerned for neighbor as for self. In the very expression of this love he revealed the inner nature of himself, as one who was not trapped by the preoccupation with the self. Jesus was not preoccupied with safety, status, possessions, or the false notion that he had made himself. We, like Jesus, discover rather than create what we are. God has created what we are, but what we do with this depends on our conscious decisions.

There is a dimension of passivity to this, a dimension of giving up, dying to the old self, but only in order to discover the real possibilities for life. Pierce Johnson has called this "dying into life."[7] John Cobb, in his excellent book *The Structure of Christian Existence*, describes the intentionality of the Christian life born out of love and the realization of the limits of the self:

Somehow, the Christian knew himself as responsible for choosing to be the kind of self he was, even when he found that his desire to change himself into another kind of self was ineffectual. Hence, he must shift his efforts from a direct struggle to alter himself to the attempt to become open to the work of the divine Spirit that could do within him something which he could not do in and for himself.[8]

Assertion of the self is essential to the life that Jesus proposed, but it is not done alone. It is possible only in relation to God.

NOTES CHAPTER III

1   Charles M. Schulz, *All This and Snoopy Too* (Greenwich, Connecticut: Fawcett Publications, Inc., 1960).

2   Quoted in John Bartlett, *Familiar Quotations*, 11th edition, ed. Christopher Morley (Boston: Little, Brown and Company, 1938), p. 708.

3   Oscar Cullmann, *The State in the New Testament* (New York: Charles Scribner's Sons, 1956), p. 27.

4   Rolf Knierim in a lecture for the Santa Barbara District of the United Methodist Church, Shell Beach, California, Fall 1975.

5   Reinhold Niebuhr, *An Introduction of Christian Ethics* (New York: Meridian Books, 1956).

6   John Knox, *The Ethics of Jesus in the Teaching of the Church* (New York: Abingdon Press, 1961), p. 22ff.

7   Pierce Johnson, *Dying Into Life* (Nashville: Abingdon Press, 1972).

8   John Cobb, *The Structure of Christian Existence* (Philadelphia: Westminster Press, 1971), p. 121.

BUT WHAT ABOUT MEEKNESS?

In our relationships with each other we must deal with vital issues centering around the concept of meekness. How long is the extra mile? Should one be long-suffering, humble, and patient? Are we to forgive more than seven times seventy? Shall the meek inherit the earth? These are the questions that confront those who sincerely try to live a religiously-based life. Just how far are we to go in our effort to express God-like love?

Many people express doubt about the marriage of meekness and assertion. They reason that meekness is always a passive, quiet, receding quality and is therefore incompatible with assertiveness, which is usually regarded as an active, speaking up, encountering quality. Although we do not know for certain where such reasoning originated, organized religion may be a key contributor to the idea that meekness and similar qualities are incongruent with assertiveness. A meek individual is often depicted as one who lacks self-confidence and self-respect, thus implying that these are undesirable traits to possess. Remember the formula for joy in the Introduction? When you continually see the sign, "Jesus first, Others second, Yourself last," hanging in the Sunday school room, you may feel confused about being self-confident. One churchgoer stated, "When I started my life as a Christian, I learned that Jesus said I must be last and least if I wanted to gain salvation." One would find it difficult to be assertive with others, to express feelings openly and honestly, to feel self-confident if one is always reminded to feel last and least. When Christians think about *meekness* it is usually in terms of being *passive* rather than *active* in life.

Kahlil Gibran reacted to meekness as a negative quality in his book *Jesus, The Son of Man*. Speaking through the eyes of Nathaniel, Gibran demonstrates how others interpret meekness as only a passive quality:

> They say that Jesus of Nazareth was humble and meek.
>
> They say that though He was a just man and righteous, He was a weakling, and was often confounded by the strong and the powerful; and that when He stood before men of authority He was but a lamb among lions.
>
> But I say that Jesus had authority over men, and that He knew His power and proclaimed it among the hills of Galilee, and in the Cities of Judea and Phoenicia.
>
> What man yielding and soft would say, 'I am life, and I am the way of truth'?
>
> What man meek and lowly would say, 'I am in God, our Father; and our God, the Father, is in me'?
>
> What man unmindful of His own strength would say, 'He who believes not in me believes not in this life nor in the life everlasting'?
>
> What man uncertain of tomorrow would proclaim, 'Your world shall pass away and be naught but scattered ashes ere my words shall pass away'?

Was He doubtful of Himself when He said to those who would confound Him with a harlot, 'He who is without sin, let him cast a stone'?

Did He fear authority when He drove the moneychangers from the court of the temple, though they were licensed by the priests?

Were His wings shorn when He cried aloud, 'My kingdom is above your earthly kingdoms'?

Was He seeking shelter in words when He repeated again and yet again, 'Destroy this temple and I will rebuild it in three days'?

Was it a coward who shook His hand in the face of the authorities and pronounced them 'liars, low, filthy, and degenerate'?

Shall a man bold enough to say these things to those who ruled Judea be deemed meek and humble?

Nay. The eagle builds not his nest in the weeping willow. And the lion seeks not his den among the ferns.

I am sickened and the bowels within me stir and rise when I hear the faint-hearted call Jesus humble and meek, that they may justify their own faintheartedness; and when the downtrodden, for comfort and companionship, speak of Jesus as a worm shining by their side.

Yea, my heart is sickened by such men. It is the mighty hunter I would preach, and the mountainous spirit unconquerable.[1]

Meekness may actually cause the religious person to hide true beliefs. We recently came in contact with a woman who had been raised by missionary parents and had attended a Christian university. Throughout her life she observed a quality in herself and in her friends that she felt hindered the full expression of Christianity. She had the following question: "Do you think that our problems with assertiveness stem from the Victorian ethic of turning the other cheek?" She also observed that many Christians seem afraid to show religious feelings or a religious approach to others (what we are terming meekness) for fear of appearing vulnerable. In other words, a Christian, once identified as such, signifies someone who is easily taken advantage of, an easy mark. Too often the meek Christian is stereotyped as one who is a doormat, a pushover, a namby-pamby, someone who is such a loving Pollyanna that he or she melts in the face of an encounter.

Must we always be fed to the lions? Meekness causes many religiously-oriented people to become mired down or confused when confronted with actual situations. The tendency is to misinterpret meekness as self-effacement and to err in the direction of leniency, passivity, and inaction. After all, isn't feeling confident being prideful instead of humble? Doesn't speaking up to someone who has offended us mean we are not understanding and loving enough? When a loved one makes us angry, aren't we lacking in forgiveness? It is no wonder that the Christian's confusion about meekness often allows another's rude and eccentric behavior.

The extreme example of a befuddled Christian is brought to mind by Joan Didion as she discusses self-respect. In her book *Slouching Toward Bethlehem*, she states:

> We flatter ourselves by thinking this compulsion to please others an attractive trait: a gist for imaginative empathy, evidence of our willingness to give. *Of course* I will play Francesca to your Paolo, Helen Keller to anyone's Annie Sullivan: no expectation is too misplaced, no role too ludicrous. At the mercy of those we cannot but hold in contempt, we play roles doomed to failure before they are begun, each defeat generating fresh despair

at the urgency of divining and meeting the next
demand made upon us.

It is the phenomenon sometimes called
'alienation from self'. In its advanced stages, we no
longer answer the telephone, because someone
might want something; that we could say *no*
without drowning in self-reproach is an idea alien
to this game. Every encounter demands too much,
tears the nerves, drains the will, and the specter of
something as small as an unanswered letter arouses
such disproportionate guilt that answering it
becomes out of the question. To assign unanswered
letters their proper weight, to free us from the
expectations of others—there lies the great, the
singular power of self-respect. Without it, one
eventually discovers the final turn of the screw: one
runs away to find oneself, and finds no one at
home.[2]

To please others at the expense of oneself is
misunderstanding meekness. The Old Testament
definition of meekness is "poor or needy." The prophets
viewed the meek as people who were oppressed, not by
their own decision but by the rich and powerful. The
meek were dependent upon God for their liberation;
meekness was not a condition to be chosen or
cherished. The meek were praised, not because they
groveled in the dust of oppression, but because they
tenaciously kept their eyes toward God.

The Old Testament does not value being
downtrodden. The blessing of meekness is faith and
hope for liberation.

The New Testament gives the same meaning to
meekness. Jesus' words, "Blessed are the meek, for they
shall inherit the earth," (Matthew 5:5) is no affirmation
of lowliness but a promise of liberation. It is a direct
quote of Psalm 37:11. Meekness is an inner attitude, a

recognition that ultimately we are dependent upon God. It is a sense of humility, a recognition that no one can make it alone. Arrogance must be set aside.

The dilemma which Joan Didion describes occurs only when the Christian believes meekness is self-chosen oppression, self-effacement. The meek from a biblical sense should look for deliverance from such oppression whether it is from external or internal forces.

Meekness leads to an inheritance not to alienation from the self. In order to see this point better it is important to consider two things: first, that meekness is *both* an active and a passive quality and, second, that true passivity comes from an ability to be active. The ability to be passive comes from a base of power. Action is a misunderstood, maligned component. Most of us do not realize that the active quality of meekness is just as much an act of love, a demonstration of Christian kindness, as the passive quality.

We will now look at three examples of actual situations in which a misinterpretation of meekness occurred. Let us turn to President Carter's sister, Ruth Carter Stapleton, for our first example. In her book *The Gift of Inner Healing*, she relates the following story:

> A friend told me how she applied this method. She was standing in line at the ticket counter at a large municipal airport. A man walked up and placed his bags right beside her. Then, ignoring the line, he pushed in front of her and asked the agent for a ticket. She said to the ticket agent, 'Excuse me, I was next.'
>
> The agent snapped, 'Lady, wait your turn.' She felt a surge of tremendous anger. Realizing this was the reaction of her inner child, she moved out of line, sat down in a waiting area, and asked the Spirit of God to help her. Her mother's unfortunate tendency to treat her unfairly had been heard in

the agent's unwitting mistreatment. With faith-imagination she 'saw' her mother and prayed for her. The moment she did, peace poured in. She then prayed for the agent and for the inconsiderate man. As she returned to the line, she was thrilled with the victory. Her mother was more beautiful, she herself was more beautiful, and the whole world was a little better place because she took those few minutes to bless instead of curse.[3]

Our concern with Ruth Carter Stapleton's evaluation of her friend's situation is in regard to her statement, "the whole world was a little better place because she took those few minutes to bless instead of curse." Stapleton does not seem to understand that one can deal with the clerk without cursing! Her friend could have come back assertively (turned the other cheek) even though she had just been mistreated. Her mother's influence needed to be dealt with independently of the situation (and perhaps she needs to be assertive with her mother also).

We need to backtrack in looking at this problem because her friend chose the wrong person initially with whom to be assertive. She should have asserted herself directly with the person who caused her concern. Instead of going to the authority first, she could have assertively stated to the line-jumper that she was there first and that he needed to go to his position in the back of the line.

The key issue is that angry or upset feelings must be dealt with so that they are not "gunny-sacked" or "stockpiled." In her moment of prayer, the woman gained insight into the reason for her anger and converted that feeling to a more controllable and acceptable one to her, but she did not resolve the feeling. If we allow our angry feelings to build, they will eventually be released, usually against self or others.

Unfortunately, the religiously-oriented person often chooses self. Repressed feelings can cause a wide variety of reactions ranging from headaches to wanting to "get away from it all" to hating self and/or others. Learning to assert oneself can help free us of anxious, harbored feelings.

Some of us are undisturbed by line-jumping or by similar slights which cause others to be upset. Is remaining silent still the religious thing to do if we are not bothered? Will the line-jumper "just know" from our silence that line-jumping infringes upon the rights of others? In some instances, the kindest thing to do, the most loving response, is not to keep still but to react assertively. By letting this person know that his line-jumping disturbed her, Ruth's friend could have *actively* taught him not to take advantage of others. If no one ever responds to him assertively, the line-jumper will remain oblivious to his inappropriate behavior. In addition to this factor, an act of assertion may actually be a protective measure for the line-jumper. If he is not *assertively* enlightened this time, he may run into someone next time who will react *aggressively*, verbally or physically.

Our next illustration involves a young woman who came for counseling concerning her relationship with her boyfriend. The two had been going together for several years, but for the past year Susan knew that she no longer loved Jack nor wished to marry him. She desired to break off the engagement and had tried to do so many times only to be met on each occasion by a variety of troublesome responses. Jack's reactions ranged from stating that he would kill himself to harshly criticizing her for not being a "true Christian," which she felt she was. He reasoned that if Susan were really faithful to her beliefs, she would not hurt him so deeply by leaving him, as several other girls had done in the past. When she broached the subject he repeatedly said how much he loved her, needed her, ending with "I thought you were a true Christian." Invariably, he would cry when she attempted to free herself.

Susan's own reaction each time these encounters took place was to feel sorry for Jack, guilty about her own behavior, and fearful that he indeed might kill himself. She felt his death would be on her conscience. Her primary worries were that she might hurt him deeply psychologically or force his suicide. She was very concerned that she do the Christian thing, which to her meant that she could not hurt Jack in any way.

Of our examples, Susan's situation is the most emotionally intertwined because of her closeness with Jack. Interpersonal assertion when there is or has been deep emotional attachment poses more problems for most people than assertion in daily interactions. Susan increased her problem by being inconsistent with Jack. She stated her feelings and then backed away from action under the barrage of Jack's responses. His responses were directed at her weak spot, her tender Christian feelings. In addition, Susan allowed their relationship to drag on for two years after she knew that she should break it off. Undoubtedly, there was some security in the relationship which she found difficult to forego, but the overriding factor was that she did not want to hurt Jack's feelings. Her reasoning was that Christians are not allowed to hurt anyone.

We feel that Susan should have stated firmly but not harshly that she was breaking off their relationship and should have remained faithful to that message by repeating it no matter what Jack said in return. We feel very strongly that assertiveness is protective. If you are not purposefully trying to hurt another, and your motives are pure, then the other person must be responsible for his or her own reaction. When Susan was told she was not a "true Christian," she could have replied, "That is not the point. The point is that I no longer love you and I am going to stop seeing you." If Jack stated that he would commit suicide, she could have responded, "I really don't want you to do that. If you have to react that way, you should get some professional help. Jack, you know this has happened to you before, and you need someone's help to figure out what is going wrong."

In any situation of assertion, one should make certain that eye contact, voice quality, and other components are expressed assertively. Susan could not look Jack in the eye when she told him she wanted to be free; her voice was weak and her words were not stated firmly. She was essentially giving him permission to manipulate her because of these failings.

Susan had proven repeatedly that she could not help Jack. By assertively, and finally, breaking free, she would give Jack the greatest gift of all—she would show him an active expression of her faith and help him to grow further.

If the breakup did incite Jack to suicide, this would be very difficult to deal with. We feel that if one knows within his or her own heart that all has been done to the best of his or her limits, then nothing else need be done. Susan was intelligent enough to get professional help. Even with this factor on her side, the possibility of Jack's committing suicide still existed. At some point, we have to let go and allow God to take over.

Our third example involves Joe and Linda, who attend church regularly. While attending a convention, they met a couple from out of state whose company they enjoyed. Upon parting, Joe said, "If you are ever in California, drop by and see us." Not long after, the other couple arrived by train, called Joe, and asked if they could stay for a few days. Not wanting to be unchristian or offensive, Joe said, "Yes, we'd love to have you visit." The couple stayed, ate Linda's "excellent cooking," and marvelled over the "hospitality" of Joe and Linda for ten days! Joe was finally forced to ask them to leave because he and Linda had plans to vacation for a week. When he spoke up, the other couple simply said, "Oh, we'll come along with you. We don't need to be back for three more weeks."

As in the cases of the line-jumper and Jack, this couple could also have been given a helpful demonstration of love through an active, positive approach to their inconsiderateness. Such a response by Joe and Linda would have given them a much better chance of knowing that they needed to change than a passive, inactive response would indicate. Joe and Linda made the mistake of waiting too long to be assertive. Generally speaking, we are more likely to be constructive in our comments if we speak as soon as we recognize our feelings. When confronted by the last response from their visitors, which most likely would not have happened if they had been assertive along the way, Joe or Linda should have firmly restated (staying assertive) that they were vacationing alone.

In these three examples, the individuals did not do the religious thing. They were not showing an ultimate expression of love. They are examples of the person who tries to guide his or her life by instilled religious principles. Most Christians are able to deal with life fairly well when it is smooth and happy, but when conflict comes they are uncertain about the Christian thing to do. Passivity holds one in good stead when all is calm, but when disturbing feelings occur, constructive skills of activity are needed.

In these three examples, the religious person ended up being stepped on and, more importantly, was not a good model of his or her faith. We believe that it is our responsibility in life to be patient with others but not to the point that we are a doormat. We must be active examples of our faith, rather than victims. Edgar Cayce says it well:

To be sure, patience, long-suffering, and endurance
are in their respective manners urges that would
lead to virtues, but they cease to be a virtue when
the individual entity allows self merely to be
imposed upon, and to take second place merely
because someone else, of a more aggressive nature,
imposes.

Then we would define for the entity what we
mean by the entity having patience—in an active,
positive manner and not merely as a passive thing.

Taking or enduring hardships, or censure, or
idiosyncrasies of others, is not necessarily patience
at all. It may become merely that of being a drudge
not only to self, but an outlet of expression from
others that may never be quite satisfying because
there is no resistance.[4]

We think that we can analyze the situations given
above in terms of "Do unto others as you would have
them do unto you." If you had been the line-jumper or
Jack or the couple who overstayed their welcome,
wouldn't you have liked to know about it in an honest,
assertive manner? Most likely, you would not have
wanted the others involved to allow you to unwittingly
manipulate them because of your silence or by your
non-assertive responses. One of the reasons that people
are not more spontaneous and open in life is because
they fear offending others. This fear is ingrained because
of the knowledge that many people, under the guise of
being polite, humble, and long-suffering, do not state
that they are offended. We suggest that, as long as one
can assure oneself that he or she is truly being assertive
in a caring way, worrying about unheard reactions is
fruitless. If we make mistakes, however, it would still be
helpful to have that information conveyed to us
actively.

NOTES CHAPTER IV

1   Kahlil Gibran, *Jesus, The Son of Man* (New York: Alfred A.
    Knopf, 1928, 1956) pp. 59-60.

2   Joan Didion, *Slouching Toward Bethlehem* (New York: Farrar,
    Straus and Giroux, 1968), pp. 147-148.

3   Ruth Carter Stapleton, *The Gift of Inner Healing* (Waco,
    Texas: Word Books), p. 44.

4   Edgar Cayce, *Circulating File on Time, Space, and Patience*
    (Virginia Beach, Virginia: Edgar Cayce Foundation, 1943),
    pp. 22-24.

ANGER WITHOUT SIN

In this and the following chapter, we will deal with
anger and aggression. We realize that many people
identify anger with aggression, but we contend that to
do so is a mistake, for, indeed, they are not the same
thing! By linking anger and aggression, one assumes that
both are bad and to be avoided at all costs. When anger
is handled in an assertive rather than an aggressive or
non-assertive manner, it is perfectly acceptable. Edgar
Cayce spoke in terms of "anger without sin," which very
aptly describes anger in terms of assertion.[1] If feelings of
anger are held inside, or if they are revealed to others in
inappropriate ways, these feelings can be physically and
mentally harmful to all concerned. (When we speak of
sin in this context, we mean hurting oneself or others
inappropriately.)

Angry feelings and the expression of anger often
cause a good deal of turmoil among those who regard
themselves as religious or spiritual. An example of this
thinking is given in the book *How to Win Over
Depression* by Dr. Tim LaHaye, a minister, who offers
five steps to overcome anger:

(1) Admit that your anger is sin.
(2) Confess your sin of anger to God.

(3) Ask God to take away the habit pattern of anger.

(4) Give thanks for God's mercy, grace, and power.

(5) Repeat this formula every time you are angry.[2]

Although possibly an extreme example of how to deal with anger, this basic attitude that anger is a sin—and that we should not have angry feelings—is too common to dismiss offhand.

We recently met a young woman who had been taught by her church and family that anger was not to be felt or expressed. She was so conditioned that, whenever she read or heard about Jesus and the moneychangers, she would try to blot the story out of her consciousness because "such behavior was entirely unbecoming of anyone of the stature of Jesus." After all, how could someone so peaceful and loving do such an angry thing? Could she be meek and loving and also acknowledge that anger is an acceptable feeling and behavior? Even those who do not consider themselves very religious often have problems handling angry feelings. Regardless of any religious or spiritual persuasion, most of us feel and act less than capable in dealing with anger, though we may intellectually understand that feeling and expressing anger is acceptable.

We do not intend to trace all the societal causes of why anger produces problems, but it is obvious that there is a belief promoted among parents, churches, schools, spiritual leaders, and the business world that anger is to be avoided in interpersonal relationships. We do not handle angry feelings and behavior well because we have not been taught to handle them correctly. If we experience anger, we either try to repress it or anguish over how to express it. Even if we express anger, we fret for days about whether we took the right approach. We have an underlying, lingering feeling that to react in anger is definitely not the religious or spiritual thing to do.

Whether we are the instigators or recipients of aggression, we are left with negative feelings once the encounter has passed. If we are the aggressor, we usually resolve to "cool it" in the future by being on our best behavior. We are unable to convince ourselves that aggressiveness is all right, since we often hurt the other person. If we happen to be the recipient, we resolve to never let ourselves act in a similar fashion; when observing that another is hurt by aggression, we vow to never again act so "uncivilized."

This response is common, but in actuality it sets up two reactions that are harmful to oneself and others. Both reactions stem from holding in feelings. It is not possible for one to be immune to feelings in interpersonal interactions. Try as one might to "not let things get to me," feelings still collect and must come out; usually, first toward oneself and, secondly, toward others.

Let us now consider an example which illustrates both of these reactions. Imagine that you are driving downtown and cannot find a parking place. After looking for what seems to be an interminable amount of time, you at last find one. You feel relief, but then a little sports car darts in front of you and takes your place even though you were obviously first! You are upset but *do not* assert yourself. You resign yourself to finding another place and finally locate one. You still feel disgruntled from the first incident, but as you shop you find all your items, which makes you feel a little better. As you finish you meet an acquaintance who talks incessantly. You need to get home soon, but this individual does not seem to recognize your hints of edging toward the checkout stand, jingling your keys, and looking bored. Finally, you escape, check out, and leave for home. After you arrive home one of your children rushes in, throws his or her coat aside, and plops down in front of the TV, knowing very well that there are duties to fulfill first.

Do you continue to hold your feelings inside and thereby hurt yourself, or do you blast out at your child? If you continue to hold your feelings in non-assertively, you most likely will say nothing to your child, give an anguished sigh or a "what's the use" shrug or a resigned grimace. Even if you do say something, it might come across as wishy-washy or pleading instead of as a direct message. If you become aggressive, you may flare up instantly, and, although you feel like grabbing and shaking the child, you give a fast-paced, raised-voice little lecture such as the following: "Can't you do anything right? You kids are just a bunch of lazy slobs! Why can't you pick up your coat the way you are told?"

The above sequence of events might take place over a period of weeks or months, but the story is a common one. It could involve a seemingly insignificant part of an individual's life—like the boss causing you little problems, or your spouse or those you socialize with irritating you. Or it could be several annoyances working in combination which cause the buildup of feelings. No matter how the sequence takes place, most of us allow our angry feelings to reach dangerous levels.

When harbored feelings come out primarily against oneself, their expression may take many forms. The result can be in the form of various somatic complaints such as headaches, rashes, stomach aches, or anxiety attacks. Although we are not completely certain that held-in feelings always cause physical reactions, they often aggravate somatic problems. For example, even though the cause of one's asthma may have been birth related, harbored feelings later in life may bring on an attack.

Other reactions to being habitually non-assertive

take the form of "getting away from it all." Strong desires to overindulge in sweets, alcohol, or drugs may result. One may escape by going to bed early or going away for the weekend. These behaviors and feelings are not always caused by harbored feelings, but one needs to analyze them very carefully. Michael Emmons recently worked with a young married woman whose sexual feelings towards her husband had been absent for approximately one year. Through marital counseling, Emmons discovered that the woman's husband had consistently told her what to do, which she had permitted by failing to respond with her feelings. Once she began asserting herself, she was amazed, as was her husband, that she started feeling sexually excited by him again. In this particular case, the woman had made no conscious decision to shut off sexual feelings, but she expressed her harbored interpersonal feelings in this manner.

It is surprising what types of feelings and behaviors can be changed by learning to express oneself positively. We have seen other problems, such as deep feelings of hate and resentment toward others and toward life in general, altered drastically by simply learning to keep life clear. Our point is that you need not let frustrations or life or anything else entangle you. Keep yourself free by taking care of your feelings as they occur.

In contrast to harboring feelings and allowing them to hurt internally, there are those who release tension in aggressive outbursts. Such reactions are harmful to others. If we yell and scream, shake our fists and stomp our feet, shout obscenities, and call others names, the message is quite clear. The emotional scars from encounters of interpersonal aggression are extremely difficult to heal. Contrary to the age-old myth that the people we get mad at end up being our best friends, we believe that it depends on *how* you get mad at them. Perhaps if one is assertively mad at another, the friendship can develop further. However, if one is aggressively mad at another, such a reaction usually causes hurt, resentment, uncertainty, and fear of future involvement. When we destroy someone there is usually no conciliation, and even if amends are made, both people are typically afraid to let their guard down completely for fear of risking another disastrous experience. Aggressive outbursts do *not* foster closeness among people.

APPROPRIATE ANGER

If harboring feelings and turning them inward is harmful, and if harboring feelings and turning them aggressively outward is harmful, what is left? Let us return to one of our examples to illustrate how to keep one's life clear and how to express anger appropriately; that is, without hurting others or oneself—anger without sin.

　　In the example given earlier concerning parent and child, let us assume that the child received an inappropriate expression of anger which we would term aggression. The reason it was aggressive is due to voice tone and volume, the use of name-calling, and the feelings involved. We are *not* stating that the child was in the right. In fact, depending upon the history involved in the situation, the child may indeed have needed an *angry* talking to. If you had warned him or her several times, perhaps an expression of anger would be appropriate. Let us say that the child had been warned several times and that you were clear of other feelings from earlier in the day. You might say: "That is the third time this week you've left your coat out, and I am really mad (said in a serious voice with direct eye contact). You also know you have chores to do before you watch TV. I want you to turn it off, put your coat away, and start your chores right now, or you won't get to watch TV at all tonight."

The threat that the child may not get to watch TV may vary depending upon what you know the child does not wish to lose. The threat item should not be something which is large or important unless it fits the situation involved. You most likely would not take away the child's TV privileges for one week for not putting his or her coat away and not doing the chores. In addition, with certain children one may use threats very minimally or not at all. Each parent needs to figure out what does or does not work with each child, always guided by assertion versus aggression principles. Finally, if an appropriate threat is given and the child does not respond, the threat should be carried through. In this instance, the TV privilege should be taken away as stated.

Let us consider one final example. In a classroom situation an individual named Tom constantly asked questions. He was not trying to impress his teacher. He was interested in the lecture material and oblivious to his fellow students who were becoming irritated with him. The class often got bogged down with his particular concerns and the other students felt cheated. They would laugh behind Tom's back when he asked questions and joke about him outside class. One person, a cartoonist, drew caricatures of him as he asked questions.

The class was non-assertive and aggressive in its expression of anger. Tom remained unaware of the anger of the class and wondered why people were cold toward him. The class was unable to proceed as it should. One day the cartoonist began to feel guilty about the hostile way he used humor to express his anger. He decided to speak to Tom.

After class he sat down with Tom and told him that the many questions Tom asked made him angry. He also confessed that he had not been very fair in the way he had expressed that anger. By drawing cartoons

he had only fanned the heat of his fellow students'
anger and put Tom in an even worse position with
them. Tom said he realized that things were not right
between himself and other students. He felt hurt by
their rejection but had been blind to the reasons behind
it. He felt bad about monopolizing class time and
indicated that he would try to be more sensitive to
others.

They talked at length about their feelings, and the
"miracle of dialogue" took place. As Reuel Howe states:

> Indeed this is the miracle of dialogue: it can bring
> relationship into being, and it can bring being once
> again to a relationship that has died.[3]

The cartoonist's decision to be assertive with his feelings
initiated the dialogue which was the beginning of what
came to be a lasting friendship.

Each of these situations we have described depict
appropriate use of anger—"anger without sin" as Cayce
puts it. Anger expressed in an assertive way can have a
therapeutic and restorative effect. Inappropriately
expressed as non-assertion or aggression, it is injurious.
Contrary to the repressive or aggressive models that our
society gives us for handling anger, we can find honest
ways to express it that lead to health and wholeness. As
Reuel Howe hints in his provocative expression,
"miracle of dialogue," assertive expressions of anger can
even be holy.

These are interactions that seem guided by the
statement "Do unto others as you would have them do
unto you." When you make a mistake in some area of
your life or cause someone to feel you have made a
mistake, there is a good chance that you would like
others to express their feelings to you. Further, you
would like the other person to express those feelings in a
wise, assertive way rather than an aggressive way. Most

of us do not want others to hold a grudge or try to get even with us or to "teach us a lesson." What we do want is honest, straightforward communication. Logically then, we should treat others in the same way. We feel that an expression of anger given in an assertive, rather than a non-assertive or aggressive manner, *is* an expression of love. Love is not only able to show itself in humbleness, patience, and the so-called softer qualities; it also can show itself in other expressions of feelings and emotions such as anger. It is a fact of life that we all behave in ways that produce reactions of anger. If we are truly in tune with our fully functioning selves, we will feel anger and very probably cause anger in others. So let us not avoid anger but learn to express it in positive, constructive ways and learn to deal with the expressions of anger from others in similar ways.

We believe that the more one grows and develops in life and learns to manifest the God-force in one's life, the less one needs to be angry—but anger and its expression will never be entirely absent in any individual. If we take the life of Jesus as an example, it is obvious that he expressed anger and caused others to feel angry and aggressive toward him. If you are doing God's will, you will be upset at times and cause others to be upset at times. Therefore, it is a good idea to know how to handle these situations in the best manner possible, without hurting yourself or others.

NOTES CHAPTER V

1   Edgar Cayce, *Individual Reference File*, compilers G. Turner
    and M. St. Clair (Virginia Beach, Virginia: Edgar Cayce
    Foundation, 1970), p. 19.

2   Tim LaHaye, *How to Win Over Depression* (Grand Rapids,
    Michigan: Zondervan Publishing House), pp. 93-95.

3   Reuel Howe, *The Miracle of Dialogue* (New York: The Seabury
    Press, 1963), p. 3.

DEALING WITH AGGRESSION IN ONESELF AND OTHERS

In this chapter we will focus only on interpersonal, non-violent aggression. We do not pretend to deal with all aspects of aggression: Our concern is with everyday aggression between individuals, which is expressed primarily by words.

Most people can learn to deal constructively with their own feelings and aggressive behavior by keeping their lives clear through assertively dealing with problems as they arise and by differentiating between anger and aggression. Once one learns that feelings of anger are acceptable and not something to feel alarmed or guilt-ridden by, then one can learn how to deal assertively with that anger. Most problems of aggression are greatly reduced if such a procedure is followed. Assertive behavior can protect you. If you are truly assertive in your interchanges, there is no need to worry about hurting others or yourself by aggression.

How do we know when we are being assertively angry instead of aggressive? Robert Alberti has discussed the differences between these two terms in his book, *Assertiveness*. He writes of four considerations:

(1) What your intention is when you react
(2) How you behave when you react
(3) What effect your reaction has on others
(4) What the societal or cultural norm is for such a reaction.[1]

If you intend to hurt another by your reaction, you would be considered aggressive rather than assertively angry. If you yell or shake your fist or lie, you would be considered aggressive rather than assertively angry. Or if the other person reacts with fear or hostility or dislike, your action would be considered aggressive rather than assertively angry. Finally, if your culture or the other person's culture or society considers your behavior to be out of place, offensive, or rude, your action would be considered aggressive rather than assertively angry.

Alberti indicates that it is not easy to answer the question of whether an action is assertive or aggressive, because the issues are complex and each situation must be evaluated individually. We would further state that each person is the best judge of his or her own behavior. This is why we feel that *intent* has to be the most crucial judge of whether an act is considered assertive or aggressive. Each person needs to decide personally whether an attempt was being made to hurt another person.

After-the-fact knowledge may cause us to alter our behavior in future interactions with certain individuals, but not our intent, if our motives were pure in the first interaction. If one is assertive, not intending to hurt the other person, but learns that the individual was in fact hurt because he or she judged the response by another behavioral, societal, or cultural norm, then one may wish to alter the behavior in the future but *not* the intent. On the other hand, there will be times when one becomes over-zealous and acts aggressively while trying to be assertive. Once again, one's behavior will need to be modified although the intent should remain the same.

This discussion naturally leads us to the consideration of how one might respond to aggressive behavior. The underlying purpose of assertion is to bring people closer together by communication, not to alienate them or drive them apart. It is important to understand that keeping one's life assertively clear day by day and showing assertive anger rather than aggression will not totally eliminate aggression. Although aggression will definitely be reduced by these two factors, there will still be times, judged by ourselves or others, when we will respond aggressively. If we are living life fully, there will be times when we overreact. In addition, there will be instances when our intent is misjudged no matter how we respond. Jesus' actions are good examples of these principles.

What should your actions be in these situations? We believe you should let your feelings be the guide in determining further action. Within this context it is wise to be guided by how you would like to be treated in a similar situation. There are times when you should apologize for behavior and times when nothing more need be said. Only *you* can determine which course to take, and it all depends on *your* feelings. If, in an interchange, you say something unacceptable and you recognize it either during the conversation or at some later point, we suggest that it be corrected.

Returning to our example from the previous chapter of the interaction with the child, we will discuss alternate responses. If you realize that you overreacted, we feel that it is a good idea to apologize. What else does "Do unto others as you would have them do unto you" mean? Apologizing when you are wrong is an assertive thing to do and not something that causes you to "lose face." Wouldn't you like an apology if someone were aggressive towards you? In the case of the child you might say: "I feel I came on too strong awhile ago and said some things that were unfair. I still feel that you shouldn't have been doing what you were doing, but I shouldn't have said all those things. I'm sorry."

Apologizing when you are wrong is perhaps one of the hardest assertions of all, but if you let your feelings be your guide in the need to act, at times you will see the need to correct your aggressive behavior. Your approach should *not* be to hang your head, drop your eyes, and sound guilty but instead to apologize assertively. It is best to handle an apology as one would handle any other type of assertion; that is, in a straightforward, genuine manner. In addition, you need not behave submissively, too friendly, or avoid that person once you have apologized. Carry on with him or her assertively in future interactions.

At certain times you will question whether you acted too strongly. Your feeling may be derived from your internal doubts or from another's reactions. In both of these instances it is good to go to the individual and discuss your feelings. One of our clients recently felt that his voice tone had been too harsh in an assertion with someone. In speaking of these feelings a few days later with his friend, he said the following: "I didn't mean to come on too strong with you the other day when we spoke. I hope things are OK with us." The friend replied, "No problem. I can really understand those kinds of feelings. We're fine. It's OK."

At this point in the apology you might say, "Good, I'm glad to hear that" or "Good, because I wasn't trying to hurt you." If you notice that, although the other person says it is OK, other cues such as eye contact or voice tone show that he or she actually was hurt by your assertion, you could say: "Are you sure? because I feel that you are bothered by what I said." The next step will depend upon the person's reaction. If the individual denies your statement and repeats that

everything is fine, we feel that you should accept it and
carry things no further. If he or she admits to being
upset, you should try to reach an understanding. From
a religious viewpoint we feel that this is the loving thing
to do. Our goal should always be to attempt to maintain
peace and harmony with our fellow human beings.

Despite this fact, with certain individuals we would
not check out incongruent behavior after an apology,
because that would be reinforcing their pattern of
causing others to feel sorry for them. It is good to
apologize briefly, but not to open Pandora's box. In
some instances loving kindness does not help the other
person.

In situations where you observe facial expressions,
voice tones, words, or other reactions which indicate
that the other person was hurt by your initial action
(though you did not feel you were in error or harsh),
you might make the following statement: "I feel that the
other night you were hurt by what I said." You then
proceed from that point depending upon the reply. Let
us remind you again, however, that some people use
hurt looks and actions to trap you, so it is good to use
discretion.

Now let us shift for a moment to a discussion of the
individual who has continual problems with aggressive
behavior. We feel that there are two readily identifiable
traits of the person who characteristically behaves in an
interpersonally non-violent but aggressive manner. The
person who behaves aggressively is actually very non-
assertive. This trait relates to the failure to keep life
clear. This comes as a great surprise to many people
because they do not realize that beneath aggression is
inhibition based on being non-assertive. The day by day
non-assertiveness of the person who has a style of
aggressive behavior is no different from that of those we
have already discussed. When such a person behaves
non-assertively over a period of time, he or she begins

smoldering inside, and for these individuals it leads to a definite habit pattern of acting out.

Since most individuals who behave non-assertively can learn to keep their lives clear day by day, the problem of dangerous suppression of feelings can be greatly reduced. For the person who consistently behaves in an interpersonally aggressive way, however, learning to keep his or her life clear is more difficult because of the second underlying trait. This trait concerns his or her basic attitude toward others. Many people who act aggressively in certain realms of their lives believe that other people are at fault and are basically stupid. In conjunction with this basic attitude is the decision that these "dumb people" need to be "set straight." Persons who behave aggressively have a strong tendency to be critical of the way in which others conduct their lives. They decide to appoint themselves as crusaders to "teach them a lesson." Because observers wait and wait, oftentimes silently building a case or collecting evidence to prove their point, their behavior comes across as "give it to them and get even" behavior. Persons who behave in an interpersonally non-violent, aggressive manner are often correct in their analysis of the other person's behavior, but they commit the greater sin with their negative attitude and its resultant behavior. We feel that reacting toward others with assertion, not aggression, provides the best opportunity to help others truly change and to correct their mistakes. This underlying critical attitude may be answered by the biblical phrase, "Ye who are without sin cast the first stone." It is not our place to judge others and to try to set them straight.

Individuals who have chronic trouble with aggression should, we feel, seek professional help. The causes of this type of behavior are complex, and experts in the field of mental health are trained to work with the problem.

HOW TO HANDLE THE AGGRESSION OF OTHERS

When someone is aggressive toward you what is your typical reaction? If you are like most people, you either fight or take flight. Receiving aggression either causes the other person to give it right back to the aggressor or to run, to get away from the situation as soon as possible without being aggressive in return. A classic example of fighting back is depicted by the following situation in which Jane, who was having a conflict with her roommate, started out assertively by saying, "You haven't done the dishes for the past four days, and it really bothers me. I would appreciate your getting them done." Rita, the roommate, obviously upset by Jane's assertion, immediately fired back, "Well, Jane, you aren't so hot yourself. Your half of the room looks like an outhouse!" Jane responded, "You dumb bitch, who do you think you are, criticizing me? Oh, you're such a slob I'm afraid to bring any of my friends into this house! And when are you going to take a bath? And what about paying me back my five dollars?"

Instead of fighting as she did, Jane could have taken the other alternative, to keep quiet and thus keep the peace. In other words, Jane might start off the same way but after Rita's aggressive comeback could say, "Oh, I didn't know my half of the room bothered you. I'll try to do better," or "I didn't mean to upset you. I guess I shouldn't have said anything." This alternative is often by default. We are caught off guard, are flabbergasted, and do not know what to say.

The behavior in the first example, in which Jane became aggressive in reaction to Rita's aggression, does not usually solve the problem but only makes things worse. The second example, in which Jane virtually kept quiet or backed off, would seem to be the better solution, but in fact is not the answer either. Although a flight response does usually avoid escalation of the conflict, still no adequate resolution is gained. Most of us who have a religious belief system or who adhere to some code of living based on love have been taught that backing off in situations like this is the thing to do—it is *keeping the peace* or *not adding fuel to the fire.* We contend that there is a third response, which points to the true meaning of turning the other cheek; it is a *stay in there* response.[2]

Instead of her previous responses to Rita's outhouse comment, Jane could have stayed assertive and replied, "Rita, my room is not the issue right now. If you want to discuss that later, we can. Right now I'd like to know when you can get to the dishes." This type of response usually allows the other person to deal with you assertively from this point in the conversation instead of continuing in an aggressive manner.

One of the authors recently spoke to a college class about turning the other cheek, and afterwards the professor came up and said:

You know, I've got an excellent example of turning the other cheek. Several years back in X (another state) my wife and I lived near campus and these college students would park in front of our driveway. Well, we put signs up and warned them several times, but it did no good. One day I was out mowing the lawn when this guy came by and started yelling at me, calling me an S.O.B., a freak, a chicken, and all sorts of names, and threatening me and was ready to fight. I couldn't figure out what was going on because out of the clear blue sky he just starts giving me hell. He finally said something about his car being towed away, so I went inside and asked my wife, and sure enough, she had called the police and they had towed this fellow's car away. Well, I was scared and decided I could either run or fight. I made up my mind it was going to be him or me, so I started to walk back out there ready to have it out with him, either he was going to beat me to a pulp or I was going to beat him to one. As I walked out, all of a sudden I thought, hey, this is silly and it isn't going to solve anything. So I got out to him and there was a stick on the ground nearby. I pointed to that stick and said, 'All right, you can take that stick and beat me up if you want to, but I don't care. You've got to stop calling me those names and treating me this way.' And do you know what? He stopped! The fellow actually stopped and left. Then about a half-hour later he walks by our house and says, 'Hey, want a beer?' I said, 'Yeah, let's go have a beer.' We did and while we were doing it the guy apologized and we had a real good talk.

Such a response by the professor was an expression of love, because instead of running away from the confrontation or trying to fight, he stayed and dealt with the situation assertively. Think about how many interpersonal disasters could be solved without hate and violence by simply *staying in there* with someone even though he or she has just wronged you aggressively!

We are not saying that you should always turn the other cheek with people. Sometimes you may need to protect yourself against distinct danger by fighting or running. You must learn to judge this for yourself. However, the best chance for a solution often lies in staying with the situation and the person. We know that the individual has hurt you and that it is difficult to stay there and deal with the problem, but we feel that such an action is an expression of love and is worth the attempt at resolution.

There are times when you receive aggression that you are quiet by default. Because you are caught off guard, you are left speechless or can only give a feeble reply. It is usually after such an encounter that the thoughts of what you should have said or questions about what the other person said start to flood your mind. In keeping with our recommendation to turn the other cheek, we suggest that you go *back* to that person and try to work out your relationship again. Once we have escaped a bad situation, the tendency is to not return but rather to either write off the other person or to be reserved and civil around them in the future.

A friend of ours was recently the victim of an unwarranted aggressive outburst and, instead of going back, decided that the other person was a hopeless case and planned to avoid further contact if possible. We understand that this is a typical reaction but maintain that it would be better to try once more to clear up the problem. We all make mistakes in life. Wouldn't it be nice to have someone forgive you and give you another chance, even if he or she had to be a little humble? We understand that protocol indicates that the aggressor should know that he or she was wrong and return to apologize (as we discussed in the previous chapter). Let us reemphasize, however, that *you* should act on *your* feelings. If the situation needs further resolving *in your mind*, then you need to initiate a new try, even though it is difficult.

ARE SOLUTIONS TO THE THEORY OF INBORN AGGRESSION ALSO INBORN?

Before completing this chapter we need to deal with one final important point. Our analysis of aggression in this book has provided only a partial answer in relation to the causes of aggression. Still we do not intend to provide a comprehensive theory in answer to this timeless question: "What causes aggression?" Many volumes have been written and will continue to be written on the subject. We are even certain that learning to be assertive is not the total solution to the problem of interpersonal aggression, but we do feel that it is a giant step forward.

One of the reasons we are not going to address ourselves to the causes of aggression is that we are dealing only with what we term *learned aggression*. That aggression is learned is only one major theory about its cause; another is that it is a natural inborn drive. Konrad Lorenz, who wrote *On Aggression*,[3] is thought to be one of the most eloquent spokespersons for the inborn drive theory. Albert Bandura (*Aggression: A Social Learning Analysis*)[4] and Erich Fromm (*The Anatomy of Human Aggression*)[5] are excellent leaders for the learning-theory approach. While we believe that most aggression is learned, we do not believe that there is enough evidence to make final conclusions about its cause. The final answer is not needed to provide practical answers on dealing with interpersonal aggression in our everyday lives.

Because we are assuming that interpersonal non-violent aggression is learned, we are presenting a way of handling this form of aggression based on a learning-theory approach. This approach is largely derived from solutions posed by Bandura and others. We are not neglecting the "aggression as inborn drive" solutions, however. Let us look at the solutions Lorenz gives to help one deal successfully with aggression, which he considers to be inborn. He suggests four basic solutions which we now paraphrase:

(1) Learn to fully understand the causes of your behavior
(2) Learn simple and effective ways of redirecting aggression at substitute objects
(3) Develop acquaintances and friendships with people who hold different beliefs or who are from other cultures

(4) Help our youth to develop zest for causes which
    are of the highest constructive nature.

We feel that each of these solutions has an active
learning component about it. To know oneself is, by its
very nature, a learning-based solution; and learning to
be assertive is one of the better enablers to self-
understanding. Each of us must learn to understand
ourself in relationship to others, in relationship to
ourself, and in relationship to God. We feel that
learning and applying assertion principles facilitates
one's growth in each of these areas.

Lorenz's second solution, redirecting aggressive
impulses, is something that must be learned. This
solution is based on the underlying belief that aggressive
impulses cannot be reduced but can be controlled, in
this case by finding substitute outlets. Our clinical
finding is that instead of having to hold the lid on one's
"basic aggressive nature," one will reduce aggressive
feelings and behaviors by learning to be assertive day by
day. If the concept of sublimation must be used, then
we believe that one of the best ways to sublimate is by
turning the other cheek as we have described it in
assertive terms.

One of the important tasks of an assertiveness
training program is to teach the student how to start
and to maintain conversation with a stranger. Lorenz's
third solution, developing acquaintances and friendships
with people different from ourselves, sounds easy but for
most of us is not a natural skill. Learning how to make
friends involves a variety of skills that are best taught in
a systematic way, such as assertiveness training. Lorenz's
third solution is also valuable, because in making friends
with people of different backgrounds, a great deal can be
learned about what is considered appropriate (assertive)
and inappropriate (non-assertive or aggressive) behavior.
If one travels to a foreign country and wishes to make

friends, one must recognize certain important differences in the way people relate.

Lorenz's final solution involves helping youth to develop zest or enthusiasm for causes of the highest nature. This must be learning-based in order to happen. Adults must help youth learn high ideals, ones that are constructive in nature. One of the best ways to do this is by being a good behavioral model oneself. This solution does not appear to be as related to assertiveness training as do the previous three, unless one believes that there is a direct relationship between the ability to be enthusiastic and feelings of self-confidence. It has been proven that assertiveness training lowers anxiety and increases self-confidence. It is difficult to be enthusiastic about causes of the highest nature without feeling confident. Combining high ideals, confidence, and practical skills seems to be an excellent way to facilitate this solution.

NOTES CHAPTER VI

1   Robert Alberti, ed., *Assertiveness* (San Luis Obispo, California: Impact Publishers, Inc., 1977), pp. 21-23.

2   We are indebted to Reverend Ernest Volkman, minister of the Community Presbyterian Church, Calistoga, California, for this interpretation. In 1972 he wrote to Michael Emmons and shared his insight into Matthew 5:38-42.

3   Konrad Lorenz, *On Aggression*, trans. Marjorie Kerr Wilson (New York: Harcourt, Brace and World, Inc., 1966).

4   Albert Bandura, *Aggression: A Social Learning Analysis* (Englewood Cliffs: Prentice-Hall, 1973).

5   Erich Fromm, *The Anatomy of Human Aggression* (New York: Holt, Rinehart and Winston, 1973).

ASSERTIVE COURAGE AND TRUST

To be assertive is to act on your convictions. It is
listening and responding to your own inner promptings;
thus enabling you to distinguish the dictates of society
from your own personal sense of obligation. To be
assertive is to be a person of authentic conscience. To
be assertive is to choose deliberately how to live. The
choices may be patterned after the dictates of society,
the church, parents, and significant experiences of life;
they may be opposed to those dictates, or they may
have a very personal base unrelated to the usual
external stimuli of life. To be assertive is to make
deliberate choices about your life.

For example, suppose you and your spouse were
driving in your car and injured a cat. Your immediate
impulse would be to stop the car and return to help the
cat. But you remember that you are already running late
for an important appointment and feel that your spouse,
who hates to be late, would say, "No, we've got to get
to our meeting." Your thoughts keep flashing back to
the cat, however, and you have strong feelings to stop.
Yet you must not be late.

What should you do in a situation like this? Should

you trust your inner promptings, or should you give in
to the "logical" arguments from other circumstances
surrounding the incident? Abraham Lincoln was
involved in a similar incident concerning a pig stuck in
the mud. One day he was riding along in a carriage
with some of his cabinet members, and as they were
beginning to cross a bridge Lincoln noticed a pig stuck
in the mud down below. His dilemma was whether he
should follow his inner promptings, interrupt the
ongoing conversation, get all dirty, and be late.

Lincoln trusted his conscience. He decided to save
the pig and told those with him that he had to do it.
He showed by his actions that he was assertively
courageous.

Cats and pigs may seem to be inane topics to
discuss in reference to assertive courage, but the content
of the actual incident does not matter because each
person will always encounter a range of difficulties with
which to deal. The cat or pig incident may be easy or
difficult for you to resolve. Possibly you may not have
feelings of stopping to help out at all. But we say that
you must follow your feelings, your inner promptings, in
whatever form they come, whether it concerns cats or
pigs or saving someone's life. The importance of each
incident depends on the person involved, not on the
incident itself.

Thomas Carlyle speaks of what we call assertive
courage in other terms when he says: "Do the duty
which lies nearest thee; which thou knowest to be a
duty! Thy second duty will already have become
clearer".[1] Very simply, to be assertively courageous,
follow your highest promptings, the things you feel that
you should be doing, day by day. And to do so, you
must develop a trust that the results will work out for
the best, even though at times it is difficult to fully
understand those results. Trust means that "the second
duty will already come clear." Learn to go beyond your

tendency to always side with your *what if* voice. What if
I stop the car and help the cat, but my spouse becomes
really mad about it? What if the cat is rabid and bites
me? What if the people who own the cat discover I hit it
and decide to sue me? The *what if* statements go on and
on, but they can be greatly lessened if one will learn to
trust. As Pierre Corneille puts it: "You should do your
duty and leave the rest to heaven." In this context,
leaving the rest to "heaven" is trusting that God's will is
best.

The question of doing your duty or following your
conscience inevitably leads to the question of how you
can know this duty and how you can be sure it is the
best thing to do. Ethicists have long debated such
questions and have, as Walter Stall has often said,
"come up bankrupt."

The question of ethics and conscience must
inevitably be settled by faith, by taking a stand. Faith is
the active way in which we perceive our world. It is
reaching out to experience and shaping our experience
by consciousness. It provides us with a ready-made
tradition from which we can draw. In the case of the
Christian faith, we know our duty from the Word,
which comes to us from external and internal sources.
The Word of God can come to us through the world,
through reading (Scripture), through speech (preaching,
teaching, dialogue), and through the Spirit (the inner
promptings, the heart).

The *New York Times* carried an article entitled
"Stealing Cars Is a Growth Industry."[2] In it a car thief
justified his crime by the utilitarian argument that he
was doing good for everyone. He claimed that he was
employing a lot of people to deliver the cars, to work on
the numbers, to paint them, to give them papers, to
drive them out of state, and to sell them. People who
could not otherwise afford a good car could buy them
cheaper. The owner who lost the car would get a new

one from the insurance company. The car dealers would be happy, because they could sell new cars. Only the insurance companies would be out, but, the car thief insisted, they budgeted for these thefts anyway. The Ten Commandments forbid stealing, but evidently his conscience does not. He believes that he is doing good for everyone, including himself.

Consider a different article by Lawrence Leitlin in *Psychology Today* entitled "A Little Larceny Can Do a Lot for Employee Morale."[3] He relates the conclusion of industrial psychologists that dishonesty on the job is personally satisfying for the average worker. They say it is a good motivational tool and relatively cheap in comparison to other motivational programs. It costs management on the average of $1.50 per worker per day. In many cases it is too costly to try to enforce honesty and to control larcenous desires. Leitlin suggests that companies weigh the benefits of higher morale against the amount it is actually costing, as well as against the costs of the traditional motivational tools. If it appears to be relatively cheaper to utilize employee theft as a motivational tool, then they should do so. Certainly, Leitlin's suggestion is much less rigorous than profit sharing, yet it could be called a kind of underhanded approved profit sharing.

Jules Feiffer captured the ethical argument well; his cartoon shows a businessman saying:

> All this big deal about white collar crime—what's wrong with white collar crime? Who enjoys his job today? You? Me? Anybody? The only satisfying part of any job is coffee break, lunch hour, and quitting time. Years ago, there was at least the hope of improvement—eventual promotion—more important jobs to come. Once you can be sold the myth that you may make president of the company, you'll hardly ever steal stamps. But

nobody believes he's going to be president anymore. The more people change jobs the more they realize that there is a direct connection between working for a living and total stupefying boredom. So why not take revenge? You're not going to find me knocking a guy because he pads an expense account and his home stationery carries the company emblem. Take away crime from the white collar worker and you will rob him of his last vestige of job interest.[4]

Is the criteria for right and wrong in these cases simply the outcome (in these cases perhaps the outcome can be deemed desirable), or is something intrinsically wrong with these arguments despite their apparent justifications?

We would answer yes; there is something basically wrong with such arguments. Utilitarianism has merit in many ethical arguments, but there comes a time when a basic inner prompting says *there is more*. Somehow, through intuition, or conscience, or Spirit, or an inner source, we know in our hearts what is right and wrong and are not dependent upon external arguments of effects or external arguments of law or social morality.

In the Judeo-Christian heritage, this is the meaning of the New Covenant, the Covenant with God which is written on the human heart rather than on tablets of stone. Jeremiah was responsible for this ethical breakthrough. He shifted the seat of ethical authority from external legal codes to the internal conscience. Ethics then became highly personal, highly individual. The Old Covenant is expressed in the commandments written by Moses; the New Covenant is written on the hearts of all human beings. This faith causes a profound trust that through our own self-dialogue we can know the will of God.

Sometimes we fail to recognize the ingenious turn of

events that Jeremiah brought with his internalization of religion. Many of us today still develop ethics from highly exterior considerations: Is it lawful? Will I get away with it? Will people accept me or condemn me for my behavior?

This kind of morality led Freud to mistakenly criticize the conscience as entirely superego-oriented. In other words, he said morality is based on what others have drilled into us. It may be internalized now, but it is society's morality, not ours.

The inner morality is not to be understood this way. Our deepest sense of good lies within us, and it is a part of us to which we must be sensitive. The conscience is also the ego, which Freud believed should actively make decisions in the formation of the self and ethics. The conscience is the whole person bringing all resources to bear on decision-making. It is, to use Paul Tillich's words, the "centered self." We have to trust our abilities to sort through our motivations, to use our reason, and to listen to our feelings. This is the kind of trust that led Jeremiah to believe that God will speak within our hearts. It led Jesus to say that God will reveal to us what we must do or say in given situations.

Outside pressures, as well as internal conflicts, often cause us to deny our conscience. We often succumb to the rationalizations of our own mind to fool ourselves into listening to promptings other than our own.

Some of the convicted Watergate conspirators confessed of knowing the wrongness of their deeds and of ignoring their consciences. In the light of their analysis of the greater picture and of what they saw as the "long run," they violated what they knew in their hearts was right. They believed that the greatest good was to protect the President at any cost, winning by any means.

The paradox of such ethics always leads to a loss, loss of self-respect, loss of conscience. Winning at any cost means ultimately that the price will be ourselves. Whenever we are struggling with an ethical decision, thinking about compromising our ethics in the present for a future "good," red flags should begin to wave. The "long run" has done more damage to the conscience than any other temptation.

In their investigation of Watergate, Bernstein and Woodward heard "the ethics of politics" repeated over and over again by those involved in the scandal. To the conspirators, the meaning of that phrase was that the standard for society is different from that of personal morality. Certainly, social situations do call for compromise in many areas, but when they call for violation of the self and one's highest values we should say "enough."

The New Covenant emphasizes inner morality, not the social morality. Social morality should reflect inner morality, not overshadow it. When Paul spoke about the external law in Romans, he recognized its validity for ordering society and our obligation to follow it, but the major thrust of his message was that we are not righteous because of the law. Jesus acknowledged the law and his intention to fulfill it but did so through love, not through legalistic slavery to law. Laws were made for man, not man for the laws. William Sloan Coffin, Jr., once said, "Laws make good guideposts, but bad hitching posts."[5]

Our ethics should be living with ourselves. Our ethical code is written on our hearts. Conscience is not just a matter of what society instills in us. It takes a good deal of trust and courage to listen to our inner promptings and to act upon them. Ethical behavior is clearly the assertion of the self and the self's values.

NOTES CHAPTER VII

1   *The Oxford Dictionary of Quotations*, 2nd ed., s.v. "Thomas Carlyle," (London: Oxford University Press, 1959).

2   *New York Times*, magazine, June 20, 1971.

3   *Psychology Today*, June, 1971.

4   Jules Feiffer, 1960. We owe this material to Robert Baum and James Randell, eds., *Ethical Arguments* (New York: Holt, Rinehart, & Winston, Inc., 1973).

5   William Sloan Coffin, Jr., Sermon at the Earl Lectures in Berkeley, 1973.

ASSERTIVENESS AND THE REALITY OF GUILT

To be assertive one must follow one's own inner feelings and act on what one believes one is called to do by the highest standards of morality or by God. Guilt occurs when we fail to do what we believe should have been done. In this chapter we will explore the subject of guilt, especially from the viewpoint of psychologists and theologians.

A young woman prisoner, S., came to Dave Richardson, who was serving as prison chaplain, for counseling. They had become acquainted during a class he was teaching on the book of Job. She wanted to talk about the guilt she felt over having killed a man.

The man had been a friend of hers, but he tried to rape her, and in the ensuing struggle she shot him. To the court it was justifiable homicide, but she was sentenced to ninety days in the Reception and Guidance Center of the prison for observation and psychiatric evaluation. Most likely, had things proceeded well during that period, she would have returned to court and been given probation.

During the ninety days, she received the message from the psychologists and social workers that she should not feel guilty for the shooting. What she had done was "justified." No one would hear her guilt for what it was, and as a result, she "blew it"; enraged, she began breaking windows and destroying things around her.

"They said I shouldn't feel guilty!—that what I had done was justified," she said as she wept. "But they don't understand; I liked the man. I didn't want to shoot him." She identified with Job who was badgered by his so-called friends. His case was different in that he was innocent, but his friends felt that he was guilty. In her case, she was guilty, but her friends said she was innocent. Like Job, she became angry with them.

S. was a warm, gentle, likable person in most circumstances, and even in her rages she did not want to vent her anger at those who didn't understand her, so she took it out on inanimate objects, windows and furniture. As a result, her psychiatric evaluation for the court was that she was, after all, a violent woman; so, rather than probation, she was sentenced to imprisonment. During her incarceration she had had periodic outbreaks of rage which, under the indeterminate sentence procedure of the state, kept her from parole consideration. It had been nearly two years since she was first imprisoned.

In two counseling sessions, Chaplain Richardson heard her "real guilt." Knowing S.'s involvement in the church, he asked if she believed that God forgives. She believed so but did not think that she could be forgiven. What she really wanted was the forgiveness of her dead friend. She longed for it but believed that it would never happen. The chaplain allowed her to leave, understanding, as she expressed it, that she was guilty for what she had done. Circumstances make deeds understandable but not justifiable. He suggested that she reflect on her religious belief and indicated some Bible passages that speak of forgiveness and justification.

S. returned a week later. She had thought a great deal about the man she had killed and about her understanding of God. As the two talked, she wept again about the man's death and her inability to say to him, "I'm sorry, so terribly sorry. Forgive me." As she was speaking, it became obvious that she was now saying the words to God and that they were authentic. In the midst of the catharsis she experienced real forgiveness.

Perhaps the case of S. and the incident surrounding her real guilt feelings seem atypical of most of our own dealings with guilt, but we feel that the case is instructive. (The magnitude and the subject of the guilt are unimportant.) Each of us is given life situations to deal with based on one's own particular level of development. S. happened to be involved in this particular incident and felt great guilt; perhaps we would not feel guilty at all or much less guilty if involved in a similar incident. On the other hand, we may feel guilty for not taking time to help our spouse with a small household chore and S. would not. There are also various degrees of real guilt. Sometimes a great force gnaws at us because of an act we did or did not commit in spite of our best urgings. In other instances, we feel a mild dissatisfaction because of something we did or did not do. Our point is that the area of guilt and the degree of guilt are unique in each person because we are individuals.

The case of S. is also instructive because it reveals some problems that many traditional therapeutic approaches cause in terms of guilt. Therapists often do not understand the reality of guilt. Since no one acknowledged her real guilt, S. began to express herself in a pathogenic way, giving in to periodic fits of violence that had been uncharacteristic of her behavior prior to imprisonment. Failing to attain forgiveness because others did not perceive the reality of her "sin," she needed to be punished and brought it on herself. When she was finally allowed to share and express the real nature of her guilt, she was able to experience forgiveness, thus ending the need for self-punishment.

Following the two sessions of counseling, S. never "blew it" again. She was paroled a year later because of her good behavior. Our experience with many persons like S., although the circumstances were often not as extreme, have led us to the conclusion that guilt is the self's way of feeling that all is not well; and it is an important motivating force for setting the self straight and being assertive. It needs to be better understood.

GUILT AND MENTAL HEALTH

Pastoral counselors, following the lead of theologian Paul Tillich, have done creative work toward understanding guilt. Secular psychotherapists have still maintained a highly suspicious attitude toward guilt, thus making it difficult for them to understand fully its reality apart from anything more than a bad feeling. Some therapists go so far as to say that all guilt is pathogenic.

Sometimes overstatement and extreme viewpoints, such as O. Hobart Mowrer's, offer the best handles with which we can grasp a problem. His human psychology and therapeutic model give us an extreme picture of human pathological behavior as guilt-oriented resulting from sin. For Mowrer, neurosis is just a medical euphemism for a state of unacknowledged and unredeemed real guilt.

Mowrer applies learning-theory to the problem and treatment of neurosis. He sees it as a *learning deficit*. Whereas other learning theorists, such as Dollard and Miller, or Wolpe, see neurosis as a process of learned excess fear responses to a drive stimulus that fails to extinguish, Mowrer sees neurosis as real guilt anxiety that results from the individual's failure to abide by moral cues. It is neither unadaptive nor surplus learning. Guilt anxiety is painful and can only be responded to by a change in the direction of behavior—a learning of moral behavior patterns.

In the Preface to his book *Morality and Mental Health*, Mowrer defends the use of the word "morality" in connection with mental health.[1] He feels that the business of the therapist is to help his client learn moral ways of behaving which will alleviate the guilt-caused neurosis. As one learns to adjust to the conscious demand and its reality-oriented adaptive cues, one is more in touch with the inner self and moves toward health.

We can criticize Mowrer's integrity therapy in many places, from both theological and psychological disciplines. That he has tied his psychology to the word "sin" is unfortunate, for it is a theological word with connotations that he is not prepared to acknowledge. On the surface, his use of the word "sin" and his suggestions for its remedy seem to fit the Christian context, but this is only true for those Christians who are legalistic in their concept of righteousness; it does not fit the ontological assumptions of the faith about the nature of sin and guilt, and it does not coincide with the concept of grace.

Psychotherapists have also taken Mowrer to task for being a moralist whose approach to therapy is not a liberating exercise but is rather a cruel reinforcement of social prescriptions for behavior. The argument rages on in a fascinating way, and yet, in spite of (or perhaps because of) Mowrer's extreme position, he has opened up an area of discussion concerning human nature that has not been satisfactorily handled in traditional forms of psychotherapy. His contribution is that real guilt is present in every neurosis, and until it is dealt with as such, the person is never really in touch with himself or herself.

One reason for psychotherapy's failure to realistically deal with guilt is its tendency to see guilt apart from the individual. The Freudian view links conscience and guilt with the superego, thus relegating it to that part of us which is *other-oriented* rather than *self-oriented*. The superego is the part of us that is learned from parents and societal pressures. Learning-theory also relegates both conscience and guilt to a similar status as having been developed as a part of the conditioning process. They are seen as intruders, available to be conditioned out of the person, rather than as integral parts of the self.

The implication of the Freudian and the Learning-theory perspectives is that guilt can be attributed to all the forces that have been at work on us from without, rather than as a state of being sensitive within the self and therefore one's responsibility. Accordingly, guilt is a result of something that has been done to us rather than something we have chosen ourself. Therefore, our behavior is something for which we ought to feel angry rather than guilty. Through psychodynamic therapy the rational ego is developed to help one see oneself and one's values apart from the superego structure, and in this sense, disavows the superego as a part of the self. According to psychotherapy, one finally gets rid of guilt through this trick.

This rational ego approach was precisely the one that was first used with S. so unsuccessfully. She was told to examine the circumstances that forced her into the murderous situation, to recognize that she too was a victim, and finally was told that she should not feel guilty. The failure, however, of this approach is that it denies the essential reality of being a person; we are the ones who make the decisions about what to do with our situations. Sometimes those decisions do not reflect what we really value for ourselves. The experience of guilt is oftentimes real, and we need to learn to own it. Therapeutic denial of its reality is a denial of the person.

While Freud was one of the first to recognize guilt in neurosis, it was, unfortunately, not possible for him to recognize it as anything more than sickness. It was a part of the neurotic symptom—ego anxiety over punishment from the superego. He regarded all guilt as neurotic and as surmountable only by the fully empowered ego. Ironically, as Freud therapeutically centered on the ego and tried to eradicate the need for defenses, he seemed to build into his system one of the most sophisticated of all ego-defenses. By locating guilt in the superego, he transferred it from the self (ego in Freud's terminology). His own theory of guilt is a projective technique. Convincing ourselves that other people make us act, that society or religion make us feel, is not much different from any other projective mechanism of defense, even if it is done in a therapeutic setting.

Freud did not give credence to the possibility of real guilt; he believed guilt was neurotic. Mowrer, on the other hand, feels that all guilt is real. Both perspectives are important if we are to understand the human condition. Freud's and Mowrer's insights are important, but it is as if each saw a coin without seeing its flip side.

REAL GUILT AND NEUROTIC GUILT

The distinction between real and neurotic guilt has been developed by many in the fields of psychiatry and pastoral counseling.[2] This distinction has made it possible for both psychotherapy and religion to relate to guilt in a helpful, healthy way.

Real guilt is an experience of pain, discomfort, or dissatisfaction following behavior that is in violation of one's own *being*.[3] It is accepted by the individual as something for which he or she is responsible and not something that was instilled from without through the learning and conditioning process. It is a violation of values, whether they be *being-values* (Maslow) or *ego-values* (the mature, rational ones that Fromm talks about). The identification of what kind of value is violated is not so important as the fact that whatever it is, it is one's own self—one's very being—that has been transgressed. This sets up a very real conflict, not between the self and society's values (ego versus superego), but between the self's behavior and its own values.

One of the characteristics of real guilt is that its content is known to us. We are aware of what caused the discomfort, the dissatisfaction and self-blame. It is a conscious phenomenon that causes one to seek forgiveness, expiation, or restitution. It can be a motivating force if it is thoroughly and responsibly dealt with. It can motivate us to reorder our relationship with ourself and the world rather than to remain in conflict (*split*). In this sense, guilt can cause a *therapeutic thrust*, to use the jargon of the psychologist, or a *redemptive thrust*, to use that of the theologian.

Guilt can, however, become a force that leads away from health or growth of the self. This is one of the characteristics of pathogenic guilt, often called *neurotic guilt*. Neurotic guilt is manifested by self-blame and dissatisfaction. Forgiveness, expiation, or restitution are powerless against such guilt. It is empowered, not only by the immediate personal reaction to it, but because of other unresolved guilt imbedded in the unconscious. A man may feel guilty, for example, about sexual relations with a woman and not know the source of the guilt—an early childhood experience of shame about being caught and punished by mother for some incident with the little girl next door. Perhaps he will confess his guilt or perform some obsessive compulsive ritual of restitution, but he will never receive more than temporary relief, thus needing to repeat the performance continually.

In one case, a man distressed by many somatic

symptoms, exhaustion, frequent headaches, nausea, and sexual dysfunction came for pastoral counseling. He had nothing substantive to talk about, but his whole manner was apologetic. He was sorry to take up the time, especially since he was not a parishioner. He claimed that he needed a minister to talk to because "psychologists were not men of God," and he was a very "spiritual man." He talked on and on about what a good man he was, about how faithful he had been in the church. He had not gone to his own minister because he felt uncomfortable in talking to him. His talk was hollow, revealing low self-esteem and a great deal of guilt, but it was all too vague to deal with.

The pastor referred him to a physician for the somatic problems. The physician referred him back, believing that the distress was psychologically-based. The counseling proceeded on and off for several months with no progress. The man seemed to want to talk, and whenever closure was suggested he would usually find some minor crisis to discuss. The sessions were characterized by numerous minor confessions and a declaration of how hard he had tried in his life to be a Christian. His guilt was reinforced each week by hell-fire-and-damnation preaching in his church.

He believed that people, especially his wife, condemned him. Her very look was the mark of censure. Had it not been for a suicide attempt in her presence, counseling would have been terminated. After about three months of primarily non-directive, client-centered therapy, he finally emotionally confessed what had really been bothering him. Years before, while his wife was in the hospital bearing their child, he had had intercourse with her sister. The weight of this guilt had pulled him down. It had gotten worse during recent years due to family circumstances and especially during visits from the sister. His wife never knew of his guilt.

The pathogenic nature of his guilt was caused by

the way he had imbedded it in his psyche, hardly admitting it to himself, let alone to anyone else. It had made a mouse of him, causing him to apologize to everyone for his very existence. His many confessions were really of little import to him in comparison; they were all he could talk about. They gave him some relief.

This particular confession was of immense importance. It was liberating to have finally shared his dark secret. He did experience some release from the symptomatic problems he had suffered. His relationship with his wife improved as he gained insight into his projective defense of perceiving condemnation in her glance. Actually she was a very accepting, warm person who cared about his well-being.

The experience of neurotic guilt is similar to the experience of marital fights in which the couple cannot fight over some immediate situation to an adequate resolution because they keep bringing up past incidents of old hurts, infidelities, and habits. The neurotically guilty person is in even worse shape than these crippled marital partners because he or she often does not even know the content of all the past violations that are brought up in his or her feelings.

Real guilt is the violation of one's own being or self. It is painful and warrants self-blame. Neurotic guilt may initially have been real, but its pathogenic character is a result of how it was dealt with. In some cases, neurotic guilt is not even derived from the violation of one's own being or self. It may be caused (here we do agree with Freud) by unexamined identification with or acceptance of external values. In this sense, we would say that superego guilt is pathogenic. It cannot serve to further growth and self-assertion.

THERAPY FOR GUILT

To deal with guilt in a healthful way, the distinction

between real and neurotic guilt must be understood. Psychotherapy which denies real guilt denies the very *being* of the one in need of help. It discourages the person from recognizing responsibility for who he or she is. Similarly, when religion deals with neurotic guilt as real, it encourages self-deception. In this way, religion gives sanction to the unexamined superego conscience or to the symptomatic experience of guilt rather than to the deeper unresolved conflict. This too is a denial of the whole person and a siding with one's internal and historical tormentors.

If either psychotherapy or religion mistakes the nature of guilt, it participates in the pathogenic power of guilt. Guilt must be seen as a signal and interpreted correctly. It is a sign that all is not right with the self, and if it is real guilt (its content is known), it can be a motivating force to set things right. The person can then reorganize behavior so that the relationship with the self and the world are not in pain-causing conflict. This is guilt resolution which comes from forgiveness and restitution. Some psychotherapists quarrel with whether the first is necessary or even possible. We would argue that it happens in most therapeutic relationships whether it is acknowledged or not.

Guilt resolution is necessary for health. Guilt's unabated presence has a pathogenic character and is observed in most neuroses. It is the business of both psychotherapy and religion to aid in this resolution. They may have quite different approaches and techniques in dealing with guilt, as well as major philosophical and theological differences, but we think there is a common denominator that is a key to the whole problem.

Guilt is resolved when one feels accepted; accepted by others and, perhaps even more importantly, accepted by oneself. This kind of acceptance needs to be full, unconditional—no longer hiding guilt or accepting the values and standards of others. Unconditional acceptance frees us to get in touch with the fragments of ourselves that have heretofore been unacceptable. The fragments are a part of who we are, for which we will not take responsibility until we experience acceptance. A new way of being (not hidden and not other-directed) becomes possible.

This kind of acceptance often happens in the therapeutic relationship between counselor and counselee. It also happens in the confession between confessor and God (the priest or minister as mediator through which it is experienced). It may be called *unconditional positive regard* (Rogers), or it may be called *grace* (theological term). It means being accepted as you are—in spite of the darkest shadows in the self or in spite of guilt. Protection is no longer necessary. The person is free to be who he or she is.

The client-centered therapy of Carl Rogers is excellent for allowing this self-disclosure in an accepting setting. Its non-judgmental approach often leads to insight. But action must follow from dealing with the guilt. If it does not occur in client-centered therapy, then we feel a more directive approach is indicated. A person who feels guilty and confesses, but does nothing about changing behavior, has missed the cue from the important guilt signals.

One of the most important steps in therapy for alcoholics in the Alcoholics Anonymous program is restitution for past wrongs done to others. One of the other key elements to the therapy is the twelfth step, which is active involvement in helping others with their problem. In the church, one of the basic parts of therapy for guilt has been prescriptions for penance. This is a clear behavioral directive.

In the *Roman Penitential*, by Halitgar (1830 edition), specific behavioral responses are spelled out.[4] For theft, the stolen goods must be restored. For drunkenness, guilt shall be expiated by forty days of bread and water (not a bad drying out process). If someone commits perjury unwittingly, he shall do penance for three years and release a slave from servitude and give alms liberally.

The Penitential is much like the Law in the Old Testament, which spells out specific restitution for all acts. It is impatient with those who seek forgiveness and then turn back a second time to their sin, like a dog returning to his own vomit (Proverbs 26:11).

Confession is not enough. It must lead the person to a change in the troublesome behavior. The value of *doing* therapies, such as assertiveness training, is their emphasis on the behavioral side of guilt resolution. They urge: "Don't just talk about it, do something!"

We like Edward Stein's analysis of the nature of guilt. It is the experience of anti-life, anti-community, anti-love, a void of being; it is hell; it is loveless life with no exit, an experience of hatred—self-hatred. He says: *Guilt begins in love, is impossible without love, and paradoxically is only cured by love.*[5] We would add only that it must also bring about a change in behavior.

Both psychotherapy and religion can deal with guilt by addressing the ego (self). When guilt is real, the person should know and interpret it as a signal for restructuring. When it is neurotic, counselors should seek ways to get the person in touch with it and then open possibilities for new being. Love and acceptance make this new being possible. Both the psychotherapist and the minister are allies in helping persons actualize this possibility.

NOTES CHAPTER VIII

1   See O. Hobart Mowrer, ed., *Morality and Mental Health* (Chicago: Rand McNally and Company, 1967).

2   Cf. James Knight, *Conscience and Guilt* (New York: Appleton-Century-Crofts, 1969); John McKenzie, *Guilt: Its Meaning and Significance* (New York: Abingdon Press, 1962); Edward Stein, *Guilt Theory and Therapy* (Philadelphia: Westminster Press, 1968); Paul Tillich, *The Courage to Be* (New Haven: Yale University Press, 1952); and Daniel Day Williams, "Paul Tillich's Doctrine of Forgiveness," *Pastoral Psychology*, Vol. 19, Feb. 1968.

3   Here we are referring to the categories of Dasein as developed by the existentialists. Perhaps we should use the *self* or *structures of existence* to communicate our meaning. We often use them interchangeably, although each has a very distinct philosophical history.

4   Portions of the Penitential are reproduced in William A. Clebsch and Charles R. Jaekle, *Pastoral Care in Historical Perspective* (Englewood Cliffs, New Jersey: Prentice-Hall, Inc, 1964), p. 150ff.

5   Stein, op. cit., p. 14.

ASSERTIVENESS IN THE CHRISTIAN COMMUNITY

In assertiveness training groups conducted in non-church settings, one frequently hears: "I don't have much difficulty asserting myself with the clerk in the store or other strangers. My problem is being assertive with those closest to me, like my mother, or my spouse, or the children." We have found two primary reasons for such statements: first, not wanting to hurt the feelings of those closest to us, and secondly, a desire to avoid any discord or disharmony in these relationships.

Close-knit church communities produce a similar hesitancy to be assertive because of reluctance to hurt feelings or create discord. Christians may tend to behave as if *keeping the peace* were more important than being honest. Even if conflict does arise there is a tendency to handle it by responding non-assertively instead of reaching an adequate resolution. Aggressive behavior does take place between Christians, but much less often. As we mentioned earlier, Christians have tended to keep the peace rather than to respond by openly hurting others through verbal aggression.

Let us now examine some non-assertive, aggressive,

and assertive vignettes in a variety of Christian
community settings. We will focus on assertiveness
examples within the congregation, in a Christian
education context, and within the Christian home. For
each area of concern we will present a situation, give
three types of response, and discuss the dynamics of the
interaction. Upon the completion of the vignettes we
will summarize the important points illustrated.

ASSERTIVENESS WITH THE MINISTER AND MEMBERS OF THE CONGREGATION

• "HOW SHALL WE MEET?"
The church service is over and it is time for mixing
socially. You observe someone who is new to the
congregation standing alone. You decide to approach
the person and initiate a conversation.

Three Types of Response
1. You wait and wait, repeatedly rehearsing in your
mind what you will say and how the other person will
respond. Just as you decide you have the ideal approach,
the person walks out the door without having conversed
with anyone.
2. You walk up to the person and begin grilling him or
her in a rapid-fire manner. The interrogation continues
without your having told anything about yourself. The
stranger appears to be ill at ease, as if on the spot.
3. Smiling, you greet the stranger in an open and
friendly manner. You introduce yourself, ask some basic
questions, listen to the responses, and share information
about yourself. The conversation seems to be enjoyable
for both of you.

Discussion
Starting conversations with those who are new to the
congregation is an important function. Helping someone

feel at home is rewarding to you and to the other person. Life is much more interesting when we are outgoing and friendly.

We encourage you to attempt the third approach given above. The first alternative (waiting and rehearsing) causes anxiety to build up. The more anxiety builds, the less likely you are to respond. Although it is not good to be impulsive, it is good to be spontaneous!

But what if you make a mistake or offend the person? And what if the conversation falls flat or there is a silence? Do not act on events that may not even take place. If any of these things do happen, deal with them assertively at that point. Life is wasted by building your present actions on what *might* take place. Follow your highest promptings; live, and *see* what actually happens. You could be pleasantly surprised.

If you do use poor technique (the second response above), refine your approach the next time. The best conversations are those that are smiling, friendly, open, reciprocal. Ask questions of the other person and reciprocate by giving information about yourself. If "dead spots" develop, relax. If no new ideas come, end the conversation.

• "BUT I DISAGREE."
You are a member of the congregation and do not agree with several important points the minister made during his or her sermon.

Three Types of Responses
1. When you reach the minister in the greeting line, you half-heartedly state, "good sermon."
2. As you reach the minister you loudly blurt out that he (or she) made two crucial mistakes today! You proceed to give an emotionally laden discourse concerning your views on the subject. Those behind you in line grow weary and the minister seems overwhelmed.

3. Upon greeting the minister you straightforwardly indicate that you disagree with two important points made in the sermon. You indicate that you would like to discuss these points further and ask for an appointment or a time to call.

Discussion
I-messages and *you-messages* differ greatly. "I feel that you missed the point on that issue" is different from "You missed the point on that issue!" In assertiveness training we teach you to own your own feelings. We do not advocate telling others what they *should* be saying, thinking, doing. By using *I-messages*, you are simply conveying your feelings without blaming.

It is perfectly all right to disagree with the minister. Ministers need feedback in order to refine what they are presenting. Their duty is to serve the congregation. The minister cannot make judgments without hearing your feelings on issues of importance to you. Move beyond roles of above and below in life. Treat yourself as equal to the minister, to the doctor, to the boss, to anyone.

Don't complain if you are not going to say anything. If you are not willing to express your feelings assertively, you have no right to complain. Assertiveness has the potential to eliminate the darkness of fear, hate, gossiping, backbiting, moaning. These kinds of reactions usually mean a fear of dealing directly with feelings.

CHRISTIAN EDUCATION SITUATIONS WHERE ASSERTIVENESS IS HELPFUL

• "YOU WOULD BE SUCH A GOOD TEACHER!"
The person in charge of the education committee at church approaches you and says, "Hello, we're looking for someone to teach the third-fourth grade Sunday School Class. Susan (the minister) and I feel that you would be such a good teacher! You surely can help us can't you?"

Three Types of Response
1. Hanging your head, you say, in a mousy voice, "Oh gosh, you don't think I would be very good at it do you? I'm not sure I would have time to prepare."
2. Frowning, you hurriedly blurt out, "I can't, I just simply have too much to do! Besides I've served this church plenty. I wish you people would quit pressuring me!"
3. Maintaining good eye contact with the chairperson, you state, "I appreciate your confidence in me, but I have too many other obligations this year. I won't be able to help you out."

Discussion
Ushers, lay readers, Sunday school teachers—these and many others are church jobs that always need to be done. We suggest that you pitch in and do your share. To volunteer to your own detriment, however, is not good for you *or* the church. In this particular situation we believe that the chairperson would not want you to say yes, when you do not want to teach. Being able to say no is a very important facet of assertiveness.

The non-assertive response (number one) is not adequate because you do not maintain good eye contact, use a mousy voice, and never answer the question. It would be easy to talk you into teaching Sunday school, but there would always be lingering doubt. Did you say yes because you could not say no?

The second response is aggressive because of the blurting out of the words and because of the defensive posture you take. You may feel pressured, but this is most often internally rather than externally caused. There is seldom cause to feel pressured and to react defensively if you have the ability, the choice, to say no assertively.

Notice that the assertive alternative (number three) allows for listening behavior. If you are complimented it is all right to say, "thank you" and *still* say "no" to the request. Although the compliment may be sincere, you need not feel obligated. Accept the compliment graciously, but still be firm in expressing your feelings.

● "DO YOU REALLY BELIEVE THAT?"
In the Adult Sunday school class you openly state your opinion about one aspect of the lesson. Several others respond by ridiculing your ideas as strange or extreme. Your feelings are hurt.

Three Types of Response
1. You say nothing further. During the rest of the class, during church, and for several weeks after, you keep reliving the experience. Your feelings of hurt do not seem to disappear easily.
2. You begin defending your opinion with more force. Your voice gets louder and louder and you even shake your finger at times. You get the distinct impression that you are making others uncomfortable and the minister asks you to "calm yourself down."
3. When you feel humiliated you state that you are bothered by the others' way of responding to you. You indicate that you don't mind others disagreeing, but it hurts to be made fun of, especially in a Christian setting.

Discussion
Each person has a right to openly express feelings as long as those feelings are expressed assertively. Ideas that do not mesh with those that are generally accepted may be frowned upon directly or indirectly. Feelings which are held in (alternative number one) do not let anyone except you know that you were bothered by the reactions of the others.

   The best way to let others know how you feel about their reactions to you is directly (alternative number three). A straightforward statement with good vocal fluency, appropriate volume and tone, plus good eye contact lets others know how you feel. It would be easy to flare up (alternative number two) at the untoward reactions of the other class members, but such a response typically causes hard feelings and causes you to feel guilty later for reacting foolishly.

Some will say that the teacher of the class should come to the aid of the person being belittled. Perhaps this statement is true, but no one else is as fully aware of your feelings as you. The responsibility lies with you to handle your own feelings. Do not wait and wait in life for someone else to stand up for your rights when you should be taking the initiative yourself. Each person must be in charge of keeping his or her life clear. If someone helps out along the way, so much the better.

ASSERTIVENESS IN THE CHRISTIAN HOME

• "MOM AND DAD, I HATE CHURCH!"
You and your spouse have two young children who are rebelling against attending church each Sunday. It is now Sunday morning, and the children are still in nightclothes with an hour before the services begin. You say, "OK, it's time to get ready to go." Your children snap back, "Aww, we hate church! It's the same old garbage everytime. We get bored sitting there. Susan's parents don't make her go! We're not going!"

Three Types of Response
1. You argue with the children, but they get the best of you and you give in saying, "Well, next time you have to go."
2. You start out explaining to the children in a calm manner all the good reasons why they should go to church. By the time you are finished you are yelling

at them, accusing them of not honoring their mother and father!

3. Because you have heard this reaction from your children many times before, and they know where you stand on this matter, you state firmly, "We've been over this before. You're going to church and that's it." If the children keep grumbling, you state, "If I hear one more word about it you're going to be grounded for one whole week!"

Discussion

The first requirement in being assertive with your children is to be firm and consistent. Children need to know where you stand on issues of this nature. In addition, it is necessary to back up your feelings. There are times in dealing with children when rules need to be backed up with threats. In alternative number three we are suggesting that you use a *get-tough* approach. And you *must* be ready to follow through on your threat in case one of the children decides to test you out. None of us likes to be the mean person and punish our children, but it is necessary at times. The more firm and consistent you are the less you will find yourself making threats, let alone carrying them out!

We suggest that when you receive regular complaints about attending either Sunday school or church that you check further. See if other parents hear similar remarks. If so, perhaps something can be done to make the program a better one.

Being assertive does not mean that you do not listen to what the other person is saying. This is one reason we do not recommend memorizing scripts for what to say when. Each situation we meet in life is different. Listen, determine your feelings; then be assertive in expressing those feelings.

Children are much more willing to deal with you if you show that you care. By listening, you convey that you respect their feelings. Of course, you still may decide against giving in to their demands.

This particular situation calls for firmness with the children. We are not suggesting that this is the only way you interact with them! Children are easier to deal with (adults are too) if you compliment them when they have done a good job, tell them that you love them once in awhile, rub their backs, participate in sports and games with them. Do not pay attention to the children only when they are disagreeing. Give them positive strokes also!

● "YOU SPEND TOO MUCH MONEY!"
The Master Charge billing came today and your spouse is looking it over. All of a sudden your spouse growls, "What's this fifty dollars for?" You indicate that it was for some clothes for yourself. "We haven't got that kind of money that we can go around wasting it on frills!" replies your spouse.

Three Types of Response
1. You hang your head and say that you are sorry. Your spouse replies, "Just watch it will you?"
2. "Well, what about all that money you spend on magazines? And just last week you went out to lunch and blew ten dollars! Don't try to tell me what to do! Oh, you're just like your mother!" You stalk off.
3. Resisting your impulse to fight back, you say, "What do you mean?" Your spouse comes back with another harsh remark, and you state, "I really needed those clothes and don't consider them frills. Why are you upset, don't you think we'll have enough money? I don't understand." Your tone throughout is firm, but non-inflammatory.

Discussion
The first response given above does not resolve the

issue. Most likely there will be another flare-up within a short time.

Fighting back, as in the second response, guarantees further trouble. Aggression typically begets aggression. If someone slaps you verbally, your first impulse is to hurt that person in return. Nothing is really settled by this type of reaction.

By not fighting back you have a better chance of resolving the issue. Our purpose with any type of assertion should be to bring us closer to the other person. Fighting back usually produces alienation or estrangement. You are trying to reach a mutual understanding, not have a fight. Do not be afraid to swallow your feelings in this situation when you feel like lashing back. But *do not* swallow your feelings of wanting to resolve the issue assertively!

An overall principle in assertiveness training is to allow each person to express him- or herself assertively. We feel that the best marital relationship, for example, is one where *both* partners can express feelings openly and honestly. So often we assume that our spouse should *know* how we feel about a certain issue. In teaching assertiveness we stress using words rather than silently assuming such and such to be true. Keep the lines of communication open. Harsh words and sharp looks close off assertive communication.

SUMMARY OF KEY PRINCIPLES

One of the important components of the assertiveness training process is to teach participants that their thoughts about being assertive may be hindering their full development of assertive responses. The formal name for this process is termed *cognitive re-structuring*. In the situations you have just read we have tried to illustrate certain key principles that will help you to rethink many of your key attitudes about being assertive. Below we have restated these important areas of concern:

A. "HOW SHALL WE MEET?"
1. Waiting and waiting to express yourself may cause anxiety build-up and cause you to be less likely to respond.
2. Assertiveness is tied together with spontaneity, not with impulsiveness!
3. Do not conduct your life on what *might* happen. Follow your highest promptings, and proceed from that point.
4. Do not give up or be a one trial learner. Try and try again, but attempt to refine your approach each time.

B. "BUT I DISAGREE."
1. Assertiveness stresses that one use *I-messages* to avoid blaming or putting down others. The emphasis is on *owning* your own feelings.
2. People are equal on a personal level. No one is above or below anyone else on this level.
3. If you do not express your feelings openly, you do not "have the right" to indulge in either verbal or non-verbal complaining.

C. "YOU WOULD BE SUCH A GOOD TEACHER!"
1. Others do not want to force you into things, for the most part, they simply react to you by the way you behave or "come across" in life. Change the way you respond and others will treat you differently.
2. Being assertive does not mean you do not listen to the other person's feelings. Assertiveness does not mean shutting off the other person.
3. You are not obliged to give in to others' wishes or demands just because they are nice to you.
4. Give others positive strokes also!

5. Aggression begets aggression. If you fight, you get either a direct or an indirect fight in return.
6. Try to make all your feeling behavior verbal. Sharp looks, ho-hums, grimaces are easy to misinterpret.

D. "DO YOU REALLY BELIEVE THAT?"
1. Responding aggressively may feel good for a short period of time, but then feelings of guilt usually creep in.
2. Be responsible for dealing with your feelings. Although it is nice to have advocates, you are the one who needs to deal with situations that cause you feelings that you wish to express.

E. "MOM AND DAD, I HATE CHURCH!"
1. Essential to successful assertive discipline are firmness and consistency.
2. Threats must be backed up by action when dealing with children. Do not say what you do not mean, or soon nothing you say will be taken seriously.
3. Do not memorize exact content for potential assertive situations. Most likely the interchange will not follow your "script"; then you will be at a loss for words.
4. Assertive messages are best when coordinated with the appropriate use of other components (vocal qualities, eye contact, for example).
5. Children need to be dealt with from a positive, caring standpoint as well as a so-called negative one. Do not be known only as "the disciplinarian." Demonstrate warmth and lovingness also.

F. "YOU SPEND TOO MUCH MONEY!"
1. Assertive communication in marital interactions is designed to foster closeness and openness, not to shut off the other person.
2. Holding back your impulse to lash out when treated unfairly is quite acceptable if you will translate

your feelings of upset into appropriate assertive responses.

3. It is possible for both persons in an interaction to behave assertively. Doing such does not end up in a fight, but rather fosters successful resolution of the conflict. The purpose of assertiveness is not to win over anyone but to attempt the best outcome for both if possible.

We feel that the principles emphasized here illustrate what being a Christian is about. If our relationships with others are mired down in non-assertive and aggressive thinking and behavior, we cannot reach our highest level of Christian development.

Now we will look at one final area of feelings and attitudes which is of particular concern for Christians. It is an area which holds us back from our highest level of development in the name of service.

CHRISTIAN BURN-OUT

In the helping professions field (teachers, ministers, psychologists, nurses) *burn-out* has been a topic of discussion. Burn-out is described as one's reaching a point of fatigue, frustration, and defeat. It is accompanied by complaints like anxiety, depression, headaches, a quick temper. Excessive use of alcohol, tranquilizers, marijuana, or immoderate sleeping are not unusual. One has reached the breaking point and—in effect—has burned-out.

What are the many causes of burned-out feelings, attitudes, and behaviors? One of the key factors is doing too much for others, being too available to help, giving beyond the call of duty, being too compassionate. The parallel between burn-out in the helping professions and in Christianity is inescapable. Many a sin comes about in the name of helping others, in the name of

Christianity. The points made throughout this chapter about service to others are crucial. But if you give too much, never taking enough time for yourself, the symptoms of burn-out will appear. Are you always available to your friends when they are in need? Do you serve on all the church committees, teach Sunday school, sing in the choir, usher, and, and, and . . .?

Michael Emmons recently worked with a client who was experiencing Christian burn-out. This person was always available to others in need. If others did not call for help, he would be sure to get in touch. He shepherded his friends and family like lambs in the fold. He was a member of several church committees and organizations in the community. He helped the Scouts, the PTA, the church. He was an expert at never saying no. All of his helping behavior was done in the name of Christian duty, of being of service to others, of expressing God's love.

He began to experience, however, the key symptoms of burn-out: resentment, exhaustion, guilt, and inner philosophical battles. He reached the point of overload. Feelings of resentment began. He hid for several days, overdosed on sleep and cut back on family involvement.

After days of burn-out behavior, guilt set in and a solution came to him. The answer, he felt sure, must be to be more loving, to help others even more! The ultimate model, Jesus, could do it—why couldn't he? If only he were more perfectly God-like he would never be exhausted, feel resentment, or want to escape. His solution was to no avail. The cycle soon repeated itself. The burned-out feelings returned.

Many of us have experienced this individual's plight. We are caught in the battle between freedom of self and responsibility to others. Where do we draw the line between Christian service to others and to our own selves?

We suggest that the symptoms of burn-out are the key. If they appear, they are a signal that you need to cut back. Less, instead of more, should be done. In this individual's case, by learning to say no assertively and by allowing others to be more independent, he was able to reduce his symptoms of burn-out. Balance was the solution. Paradoxically, by being in better balance he was able to be of higher quality service to others!

OUT OF THE SHADOW OF MAN

Often religion has been cited as a bastion of male supremacy, doing as much as or more than any other institution in society to keep women from being assertive. A main feminist criticism of religion has been its sanctioning of non-assertive roles for women. In this chapter we will examine the biblical understanding of women and suggest ways that assertion for women can be seen in the context of faith.

WOMAN IN THE SHADOW OF MAN

Rowland Wilson has a cartoon picturing Adam standing in the Garden of Eden. He is surrounded by animals with the snake entwined in a tree behind him. Across the garden walks Eve. Adam, startled by the newcomer, says, "Who's the new man?"[1]

This cartoon captures the biblical view of women—they were viewed from the perspective of man. They were, as Old Testament scholar Phyllis Bird puts it, "adjuncts of men."[2] In other words, they were important and good only as they were seen as helping, supporting, or satisfying men. A good woman was the shadow of a man.

The woman had a place in society so long as she was attached to a household headed by a man. She was considered property. She was bought and sold into marriage by the traditional wedding gift to her father. One of the commandments prohibited coveting a neighbor's property, his house, servants, ox and ass, and his wife.

The woman's role was to give to her husband sexually, to bear children, preferably boys, and to take care of the household. It was a curse and a great failure if she was barren. Adultery was an issue of property rights and authority; thus it was a crime only for a woman. She could be put to death for it. The value of a man's property was demeaned by adultery and his authority challenged. For the same reasons, a woman's virginity was important before marriage.

The Hebrews were not prudes about sexuality, but they were jealous of their property. Extramarital sex was not uncommon. Men sought out prostitutes; however, the prostitutes were not given much status in society, for they were outside the protective bounds of marriage. Rape was also viewed primarily as a property issue. The girl's father was compensated duly by payment, and the offender married the girl.

A woman was excluded from the sociopolitical realm of society as well as the religious. Only under the protection of her father's or husband's household was she protected fully by the law and allowed to participate in society. Special sanctions were given to widows as the Levirate Law, which provided the widow with her deceased husband's brother in a new marriage. A woman had no property rights of her own. She could not inherit property. Woman *was* property.

Life was not easy for a woman in ancient Israel. One of the prayers of thanksgiving still used in orthodox synagogues is a thanksgiving to God, "who has not made me a Gentile, a slave, . . . or a woman."

Lest we get too sorrowful for women in ancient Israel, we ought to remind ourselves of women in America. Georgia Harkness calls our attention to a letter from Abigail Adams to her husband, John, written in 1777:

> In the new code of laws which I suppose it will be necessary for you to make, I desire you would remember the ladies and be more generous to them than your ancestors . . . . If particular care and attention is not paid to the ladies, we are determined to foment a rebellion, and will not hold ourselves bound by any laws in which we have no voice or representation.[3]

Apparently, John did not take her revolution seriously because no laws generous to women came. Our Constitution and Bill of Rights, much like the law of the Old Testament, does not give women much consideration. Women were not deliberately excluded from protection of their rights as were the slaves; they just were not considered. Rights were extended to them more in keeping with the cultural practices of the day than through constitutional guarantees. The best way to secure the rights they had was through male protectors—by attachment to the household of father or husband.

THE RIBBING OF ADAM

There are two creation stories in Genesis. In the first story (Genesis 1:1-2:4a) man and woman are created simultaneously. The second begins in Genesis 2:4b and is older than the first creation story. In the second story Adam takes the ribbing, and thus woman is created. God causes a deep sleep to come upon Adam and then takes his rib and fashions a woman.

The story is an aetiological legend, meaning that it is a legend by which ancient people explained how events began. It explains, for example, place names, why serpents crawl on their bellies, and why people are naturally afraid of them. It explains why serpents bite one on the heel and why they must have their heads crushed if they are to be killed. An explanation is given for why women suffer in childbirth and why men must work by the sweat of their brow. Explanation is given for why people do not have ribs all the way to their hip. (God removed one to form woman.) Sexual desire, for example, is powerful because woman was originally taken from man's flesh, leaving strong urgings for flesh to be united again. Woman is "bone of my bone, flesh of my flesh," and for this reason the man "leaves his father and mother and cleaves to his wife and they become one flesh" (Genesis 2:24).

We can see in these statements an explanation for male dominance and female passivity. Man was created first, even before plants and animals. This explains his authority. Other religions have similar creation myths explaining male dominance. The Japanese creation story, for example, has woman (Izanami) speaking first after their creation and thus giving birth to an imperfect child. The two have to start all over again and the second time man (Izanagi) speaks first and a healthy child is born.

In the second Genesis narrative, after God had created man, God saw that it was not fit that man should be alone, so he made the other creatures. Gerhard Von Rad equates this aloneness with "helplessness."[4] The other creatures were thus viewed as helpmates, but they were not enough, so woman was created.

One can understand the need for women to be manipulative, rather than assertive, in a social structure that has kept them second class citizens. Just as blacks learned to shuffle for whites, so women learned to use wiles as the technique for getting along.

The woman was created as an afterthought, after all other creatures. She was a helpmate fit for man, but temptation came immediately. Woman was tempted by the serpent, ". . . you will be like God" (Genesis 3:15). How tempting for one of low station to be higher than what the givers of life have provided! She invited the man to join her, but they experienced the Fall. The truth of the story is powerful; any persons unable to accept themselves for who they are will stumble and fall. No one should seek to be God.

When called to account for their actions by God, man blamed woman. Man could not assert himself by bearing his own responsibility. Georgia Harkness calls this the first case of hiding behind a woman's apron strings.[5] As so often happens in non-assertive behavior, man sought a scapegoat for his own feelings.

Phyllis Bird suggests that the "helper fit for man" ought not carry negative connotations. "Helper" as it comes to us in the Hebrew language used here does not carry status connotations. It literally means a helper *opposite* or *corresponding* to him.[6] Nevertheless, the status connotation has been given in traditional interpretations of the passage. Bird offers a helpful corrective, but the story has served as an explanation of the station of woman in Hebrew patriarchal society; she was subject to man. The story did not lead to the subjection of women; it represented a reflection of the cultural fact that ancient Israel was a patriarchy. Women lived in the shadow of men. They were to help, obey, and satisfy men.

THE NEW TESTAMENT VIEW OF WOMEN

In "The Diary of Adam and Eve" Mark Twain pictures a frustrated Adam not knowing what to do with woman. "This new creature with the long hair is a good deal in the way. It is always hanging around and following me about. I don't like this; I am not used to company. I wish it would stay with the other animals."[7] Adam's perplexity with woman reflected the position of many individuals in the New Testament. The early days were during a time of transition from the *law* of the Old Testament to the *grace* of the Christian movement. The Christians inherited the traditional patriarchal laws of the Old Testament, but it was obvious that things were in a state of flux. The old roles, the old prescriptions, did not fit well with the radical emphasis on love in Jesus' teachings. The disciples knew how Jesus treated women. Many women gathered around him, and he treated them with dignity as persons. The disciples knew what Christian liberty called them to do, but they also knew how they had been accustomed to treating women. They were not quite sure what to do with the women.

The New Testament struggled with a new ethic, but it did not come easily. In some cases it came to a position that was even harder on women than those of the Old Testament. In I Timothy we are told that Adam was not deceived, it was Eve; she became the transgressor (2:14). She was definitely not to assert herself, "Let a woman learn in silence with all submissiveness. I permit no woman to teach or to have authority over men" (I Timothy 2:11-12).

The Apostle Paul agreed with this teaching on silence and also wrote that a woman should cover her head upon entering a church; otherwise she would dishonor herself. He believed that "if they have anything they desire to know, let them ask their husbands at home. For it is shameful for a woman to speak in church" (I Corinthians 14:35).

A story is told of a four-year-old boy in church being told by his sister not to talk in church. "Why can't I talk?" asked the boy. "They won't let you," replied the sister. "Who won't let me?" asked the boy. "The hushers," said the little girl. Apparently, the "hushers" were at work in Paul's day too, but they were hushing women as well.

Perhaps a historical word is in order here to better understand the hushers. Their mistake was that they were unable to distinguish between the women of the faith and the women of the streets, the hustlers of Corinth. In their time the high-class prostitutes of the city, the *heterae* who walked in public unveiled, were regarded as a disgrace. They spoke without hesitation, for they had no husbands to keep them quiet or talk for them. It was customary, on the other hand, for women of good repute to remain secluded and for the most part uneducated. Paul did not want the women of the church to be mistaken for women of the streets. His words show a clear cultural bias.

Paul, as with all his contemporaries, was a man of his culture. And even though his conversion made a new creation of him, we must remember that subconscious prejudice dies slowly. Certainly Paul's having been a Pharisee, the strictest of Jews, made breaking with traditions concerning women exceedingly difficult. Nevertheless, he did struggle against it, and we do find some marvelous, liberating words from him that stand in direct contradiction to some of the attitudes we have examined so far. We will look at these words later in the chapter.

Let us summarize first by saying that though the New Testament represented a time of transition and question as to the place of women, it primarily reiterated old traditions and attitudes. Women were viewed in the shadow of men.

WOMEN AS ASSERTIVE PERSONS

A woman cannot easily gain insight into how she ought

to become an assertive woman from the Bible. The scriptures tell a woman to be *un*assertive. She should be submissive. There are still books on the market these days that draw heavily upon scripture to prescribe the roles of women. The problem is that these books are culture-bound. They are anachronisms, forcing intolerable positions upon women. In them is much *proof texting*, which means picking and choosing the scripture that authors want women to abide by. They advocate remaining true to the Bible, while actually rejecting many laws and examples that at one time were sanctioned in the Bible. One can hardly hold up Sarah as an example of feminine behavior. Her husband, Abraham, discovered that Pharaoh desired her, so for the safety of them both he lied and said she was his sister. She thus went to live with Pharaoh, complacent and loyal to her husband's deceit, while he made his fortune.

The truth of the matter is that everyone rejects some of the cultural baggage of biblical stories. No one lives by the letter of the law, no matter how biblical one claims to be. The real question of biblical exegesis is understanding the story in its own context and then determining how it can be translated into a different culture.

If one should not determine how to be a woman from the scriptures, what should be the role of the Bible in this quest? We believe that a modern woman should go to the scriptures to determine how to be a *person*. It is the same reason a man reads the Bible. This is the key to unlocking the Bible in reference to assertion.

Whenever stories of the Bible emerge with memorable accounts of women, it is not just the shadow of a man that is shown. What we see is a real person, a person of character, of persistence, of loyalty and love. It is a person who knows what she wants and is not afraid to assert herself.

Both Deborah and Miriam are remembered as *prophetesses* or *judges* for the ancient Hebrews, helping to motivate the people in their courageous attempts to establish themselves in their own land. The Song of Miriam and the Song of Deborah are two of the oldest strands of Hebrew poetry in the Bible. They were women in their own right, not just as the culture molded them.

An example of an infamous assertive woman was Jezebel. Her husband, Ahab, could not make up his mind or act assertively. Unfortunately, she was irresponsible in her use of power and brought tragedy to herself and others. Assertion must consider the rights of others.

Abigail, concerned about her husband who was foolish in refusing to allow David and his men to join in the harvest festivities, went to David and pleaded her husband's case. He was, after all, what his name Nabal indicated, a fool. When Nabal awoke the next morning from his drunken stupor and realized that his wife had saved him from his own foolishness, his spirit left him. He died soon after.

In the Elisha stories, which were meant to enhance the reputation of Elisha as a wonder worker, a woman emerged as a person of real character. Holding her son's head to her bosom, staying beside him even in death, the Shunammite woman showed the persistence and power of care. She had love that outshone all the miracles of wonder workers. In the folklore of world literature the heroic deeds of men often are the center of attention. Exploits of male heroes like Elisha make good stories, but they never touch the heart like a mother's love. The woman refused to give up her child even after his death. She went to Elisha and demanded that he bring the boy back to life. Elisha had predicted the birth of her son in the first place; he then brought him back to her.

When we turn to the New Testament, how can we read without being moved by such a person as Mary Magdalene, who departed from the usual prescribed role of a woman and yet who was commended by Jesus? Perhaps to the Hebrews the only women who counted were the obedient, passive ones, but to the modern reader the woman who really counts is the woman of character. Mary, Deborah, Abigail, Miriam, and the Shunammite woman refused to be merely the shadows of men. They were assertive persons who took a stand toward life.

THE CHRISTIAN LIBERATION OF WOMEN

Paul was not the woman-hater some people believe. He was breaking from a strict past, and so contradicted himself at times. In actuality, Paul did allow women to speak in the churches. They prophesied and prayed. According to Acts, they also took part in the breaking of bread, something that was later denied them. Paul worked closely with women. Dare we say some of his best friends were women? Women were an essential part of the early church, and without their leadership the church would have had an even more difficult time. Women provided their homes for worship. Some were deaconesses. Dorcas was called a disciple in the only New Testament reference in which the word appears in its feminine form.

Jesus had set the stage for this radical departure in the treatment of women. He treated them as individuals just as he did tax collectors, Romans, and demoniacs. Jesus accepted people for who they were—all God's children. He told them about God's all-accepting, unconditional love. This enabled them to look into themselves, to love themselves, and to be themselves with a new sense of dignity. Knowledge of this love brought a new being and a new way of doing things. It was an experience of new birth. We analyzed earlier how this affected such persons as Zacchaeus; the same was true for women.

Unfortunately, first-century culture still viewed people by station and role. Labels were important—Gentile, Pharisee, Samaritan, Jew, slave, publican, sinner, man, and woman. Each label had a certain prescribed way of relating attached to it, and when Jesus did not relate according to these prescriptions he was criticized. In remaining person-centered rather than culture-bound he brought a contagious excitement to people who experienced a sense of liberation.

In Luke's gospel, the Mary-Martha story tells us of Martha's complaint to Jesus that she was having to serve in the kitchen while Mary sat, learning at Jesus' feet. She said in effect, "Lord, don't you care that she's left me alone? Tell her to get in here and help me." Her plea was that Mary know her place, her station as a woman. The men were to listen and the women were to serve. "Martha, Martha, you are anxious and troubled about many things, one thing is needful. Mary has chosen the good portion, which shall not be taken away from her" (Luke 10:41-42). Jesus saw Mary as a person, not as a role.

When the woman of the street anointed Jesus' feet and wiped them with her hair, the Pharisees were certain that he would throw her out, for that was what was expected of a decent man. He did not, and as some of the accounts show, the disciples were upset by it. Jesus had her continue with the anointing, thus using the opportunity to teach about love and forgiveness, saying essentially, "Leave the woman alone. She hasn't ceased to kiss me since I came, but you haven't bothered." Perhaps the disciples felt guilty about this act of compassion, which contrasted with their own sense of propriety that prevented them from such gestures. They

may have heard Jesus' message as advocating an end to
male projection of guilt onto women. Perhaps they
heard it as a command to stop telling women what they
could and could not do. Certainly they must have
understood him to say that people needed to do more
loving and less judging.

At the crucifixion the women provided the
community of believers with the greatest stability. They
stayed with Jesus at the cross and visited the tomb,
while the disciples hid, denied their loyalty, or went off,
disillusioned.

Paul finally penned the meaning of the new-found
freedom for men and women as they encountered Jesus.
In his letters he wrote about Christian liberty, the
Christian liberation that came with the experience of
grace—God's unconditional love. In reality, this broke
down all distinctions and barriers. "For in Christ Jesus
you are all sons of God. . . . There is neither Jew nor
Greek, there is neither slave nor free, there is neither
male nor female; for you are all one in Christ Jesus"
(Galatians 3:26-29).

Unfortunately, the cultural ramifications of
Christian liberty were too broad and too sweeping for
all aspects to be realized in the beginning. As Whitehead
puts it, "So slow is the translation of an idea into
custom."[8] Jesus did not spell out the social implications
of his love. He simply acted out his faith in decisive
ways; his culture was not ready for this, so they killed
him.

Christians took 1800 years to recognize the
implications of Christian liberty for the question of
slavery. John Wesley was astonished that his friend and
colleague Whitefield could, on the one hand, preach
God's love and, on the other hand, receive slaves to be
bought and sold. It was easy for Whitefield, for it had
been done for so long.

Christianity took 1900 years and more to recognize

the implications of Christian liberty for women. Grace even breaks the bondage of cultural prescriptions which originate in the Bible. The God of Grace is not interested in performance. God is interested in persons. The God of Grace is not interested in roles, in submissiveness, in woman as the shadow of man. God is interested in persons who have a perfect right to assert themselves, who have a perfect right to be themselves. The assertive woman is in conflict only with the cultural demands of ancient Israel, she is not in conflict with God's grace. The assertive woman is the fulfillment of grace.

Grace calls for decision, for decisiveness. In ancient Israel decision was very important too, but it was a man's decision not a woman's. Joshua made his call to Israel saying, "Choose today whom you will serve . . . as for me and my house we will serve the Lord" (Joshua 24:15). He chose for his women. The New Testament also demands decision, but no one chooses for someone else. Each person—man and woman—is responsible for himself and herself. The New Testament represents a change from the Old Testament in the perspective on woman, just as the first creation story differs in perspective from the second one in Genesis. From the New Testament perspective, failure to respond with one's own personal decision is the greatest tragedy of all. Indecision and non-assertiveness cause us to be lost. Faith is an act; it is taking a stand toward life and accepting responsibility for oneself. A man cannot make such a decision of faith for a woman. The assertive woman is the product of grace.

NOTES CHAPTER X

1   Rowland B. Wilson, *The Whites of Their Eyes* (New York: E. P. Dutton and Company, Inc., 1962), p. 7.

2   Phyllis Bird, "Images of Women in the Old Testament" in Rosemary Radford Ruether, ed., *Religion and Sexism* (New York: Simon and Schuster, 1974), p. 41.

3   Quoted in Georgia Harkness, *Women in Church and Society* (Nashville: Abingdon Press, 1972), p. 87.

4   Gerhard Von Rad, *Genesis: A Commentary* (Philadelphia: The Westminster Press, 1961), p. 80.

5   Harkness, op. cit., p. 154.

6   Bird, op. cit., p. 73.

7   Mark Twain, "The Diary of Adam and Eve," *The Complete Short Stories of Mark Twain* (New York: Bantam Books, 1957), p. 273.

8   Alfred North Whitehead, *Adventures of Ideas* (New York: The Free Press, 1967), p. 50.

ASSERTIVENESS AND THE RESPONSIBLE SELF

A mother overheard her daughter and son arguing about a doughnut left from breakfast. They did not want to split it and could not decide who should have it. In exasperation her son finally blurted out, "One of us ought to act like a Christian about this; I think it should be you." Implicit in this statement is a definition of Christian behavior: a Christian looks out for the interests of others.

The boy was incorrect, of course, in his use of the definition, but it is a difficult task for even the most sophisticated mind to know how to apply this definition to the Christian life-style. That the definition is a prescription for Christian behavior is clear in the Apostle Paul's statement, "Let each of you look not only to his own interests, but also to the interests of others" (Philippians 2:4). In this chapter we would like to explore the meaning of this altruistic dimension of Christianity and its implications for assertion.

The context for Paul's words was a letter to a church that he dearly loved. He had praised it for its effectiveness, and then he saw it threatened by internal rivalry stemming from petty jealousy over honors and rewards—the age-old problem of one-upmanship, boastfulness, and envy.

It is easy to fall prey to the temptations of pride, which move us from health and assertive self-respect to extreme self-absorption. In a *Peanuts* cartoon Linus is pictured sitting with Charlie Brown telling of his good intentions for the future.

> When I get big I'm going to be a humble little country doctor. I'll live in the city see, and every morning I'll get up, climb into my sports car, and zoom into the country! Then I'll start healing people. . . . I'll heal everybody for miles around! I'll be a world famous humble little country doctor.[1]

We are often trapped into thinking more about ourselves than about others or about the tasks that are important to us. It trips us up. Musicians play much better when they lose themselves in their music. When they begin to think about themselves and the spotlight that is on them, they make mistakes. If athletes focus on how they look rather than on the performance of their particular sport, they do poorly. Charitable organizations are often most effective in their earliest phases, before a large percentage of funds is needed for self-perpetuation.

The people of Philippi were in trouble. The congregation did many good things, but as they praised themselves they began to fight for honors. Assertive life-styles became entangled in jealousy and rivalry. Their own preoccupation with themselves had gotten in the way of their task, that of being the church.

Paul witnessed the rift in the community of believers and suggested that if there is "any encouragement in Christ, any incentive of love, any participation in the spirit, any affection and sympathy, . . . have that same love." (Philippians 2:1-2).

One needs special understanding of Paul's word *love*.
The Greek word for love here is *paraklasis*, which means
literally "one whom you call to your side." In Latin it is
translated "advocate." It is one who is a comforter,
helper, and strengthener. A good relationship is not one
which brings down, demeans, or undercuts, but one
which brings support. A friend is one whom you would
call to your side in time of need.

An assertive living atmosphere is one that is not
suspicious and where people can be less defensive and
self-absorbed. It is one where you do not need to be
guarded, and one which does not force competition. It is
an atmosphere where people are advocates for one
another.

Paul continued, "Do nothing from conceit or
selfishness, but in humility count others better than
yourselves" (Philippians 2:3). This does not mean we
should deprecate ourselves, for that kind of humility is
usually not sincere. He cautioned us against narcissism
and grandiosity. Frank Kimper, formerly a counseling
professor at the School of Theology in Claremont,
California, says that he understands even the worst
cases of inferiority complexes as having, beneath the
surface, a basic "rage because people didn't think highly
enough of them." Psychiatrist Camilla Anderson says
that humility and inferiority are not the real source of
people's problems. The great crippler and source of
mental disorder beneath even humility is grandiosity.

Humbleness can be vanity. Recall Linus who would
be the "greatest humble country doctor in the world."
Paul did not advocate non-assertiveness through false
assessments of ourselves or the devaluing of our own
self. He was concerned about outward claims of
distinctions. Don't spend your time seeking honors,
rewards, and recognition. That will get in the way of the
very thing you seek to do.

Paul understood the disciplinary value of counting

others better than ourselves. It does not come
naturally, yet it is good, provided it is done properly.
There is a basic narcissism deep within us all. Secretly,
at least, each of us thinks of ourself as a little better
than the next person, and we have to stand outside
ourselves to see things in a proper perspective. We give
ourselves deferential treatment and consideration.
Therefore, it takes considerable effort and discipline to
view ourselves properly in relation to other persons.
From our own viewpoint we are number one, but in
reality we are one among many.

Paul recognized that for us to see this reality we
must consciously attempt to count others better than
ourselves, or as the King James Version translates,
"Esteem others better than yourself." In other words, it
is better to hold up and praise others, being their
advocate, than to spend time tooting one's own horn.

We like the King James Version, "esteem others." It
is very positive. We wonder why it is so often
interpreted in such a negative way—as a put-down of
oneself. In the gospel message we are all important.
Everyone is loved by God. This particular passage does
not point to self-effacement but to the recognition that
others have their importance and their good points. We
need to truly recognize them, not begrudge them. It
seems that Paul, in his awareness of self-preoccupation,
knew that this could happen only by intentional
elevation of others in our esteem.

When we can rejoice in another's good fortune, we
have experienced a kind of love that is beautiful, that is
of Christ. We then can be advocates for others as Christ
was. This was Paul's meaning. It was not that we should
put ourselves down, for certainly Paul was not one to
denigrate himself. He was proud of who he was and
what he had done. More than once in the book of Acts
and in his letters he recounted for his listeners the
heroic story of his life.

Perhaps the most important words from this passage in Philippians are, "Let each of you look not only to his own interests, but also to the interests of others" (Philippians 2:4). Paul touched on the most important aspect of community and humanity, which is altruism. There have been debates for centuries among ethicists, psychologists, and philosophers about the possibility of altruistic behavior. We believe it is rather sophomoric to argue that behavior is only egotistically motivated. Certainly there is a "pay-off" or reward for most behavior, even behavior for the benefit of others. While personal satisfaction is part of the reason for looking out for the needs of others, this does not negate the reality of altruistic thrusts in our motivation and behavior.

In our world, which stresses individualism and "doing your own thing," we easily lose sight of community. The results are alienation and loneliness. In the elusive search for self, many have failed to see that the self is made in relationships. Self-discovery and realization have become self-preoccupation, hiding the great paradoxical discovery of religion: that by self-denial or losing the self one truly finds the self. Altruism is a dimension of this discipline of discovery. As the Hindus and Buddhists discovered, only when one ceases craving and striving after rewards and gain does the greatest reward come.

Jane Goodall excited the world of anthropologists and zoologists when she discovered that chimpanzees would look to the needs of others by sharing food. Chimps are to some extent a communal animal, although much less so than humans. When she saw this behavior among them, she came to realize that it was not aberrant behavior. They were being "good chimps," what chimps ought to be, a communal animal responsive to the needs of others.

It is rather ironic that Goodall's discovery needs to be rediscovered in man. When we are responsible for

others, when we are looking after the needs of others,
we are really only being what we ought to be, being
good people. We discover what it means to be a person.
We discover, as John Donne puts it, that "no man is an
island." We discover something about us. Walter Stace
describes this in an almost mystical way when he
suggests that morality is the realization that what we do
to others we really do also to ourselves. Jesus understood
this also when he said, "As you did it to one of the least
of these, my brethren, you did it to me." (Matthew
25:40).

When we are selfish and conceited we particularize
our need. This means that we miss sight of a large
dimension of our being, our communal nature. There is
a real sense in which, as Stace says, our need is our
neighbor's need and our neighbor's need is our
need.[2] We capture this awareness not by self-
depreciation, but by honestly lifting up others and being
advocates for them, and by supporting and caring for
their needs. Paul and Jesus seemed to recognize this
common self that is part of us all. They called it *Spirit*;
some call it *Unity*; others *Transpersonal Self*, others
Atman. Regardless of the words used, the self is best
served and asserted in a real way when it is responsible
and caring for the needs of others. This strengthens our
relationships and brings joy. It brings self-discovery, and,
as Paul says, this is the way to experience the mind of
Christ.

NOTES CHAPTER XI

1   Charles Schulz, *You're a Winner Charlie Brown* (Greenwich,
     Connecticut: Fawcett Publishers, Inc., 1966).
2   "The Foundation of Ethics," McGraw-Hill Sound Seminars.

ASSERTIVENESS TRAINING AND CHRISTIAN COUNSELING

"What therapeutic approaches should I use in my counseling?" is a recurrent question of the clergyman or pastoral counselor. Many different therapies are available these days. Should the counseling procedure be eclectic, molded to the type of person or problem that is being presented? Are some therapies more consistent with the Christian message and perhaps some incompatible with it?

A number of excellent books answer these questions.[1] Some writers have suggested that the Christian approach to therapy is to think carefully about one's own theology and to choose consistently only the therapeutic methods that are in line with it. Others have suggested that we should not be hung up on the underlying theoretical discussions and should choose whatever therapy works for the good of the person.

Among the major works in the field of psychotherapy and religion we find very little discussion of the newer behavioral approaches to therapy, such as what is broadly known as Behavioral Modification, and none discussing assertiveness training. Pastoral counselors have been uncomfortable with behavioral approaches to therapy, and yet these approaches are gaining wide recognition in the secular field and are proving to be very effective. We would like to suggest that assertiveness training can be used in the Christian context, consistent with theological considerations.

KNOWING, BEING, AND DOING

In an excellent article, "Pastoral Care and Counseling in Biblical Perspective," William Oglesby distinguishes three possible styles for pastoral counseling.[2] Each style has a different focus centering on: (1) *right knowing*, (2) *right being*, or (3) *right doing*. Of the three, the first two enjoy the most popularity and use among pastoral counselors.

Counseling that emphasizes right knowing has been based on the approaches of Albert Ellis' *Rational Therapy*, Viktor Frankl's *Logotherapy*, *Transactional Analysis*, and *Psychoanalysis*. If we know ourselves and our values and are freed from blocks to self-awareness, we will change ourselves and our behavior.

The counselors who emphasize right being suggest that knowing and doing ultimately depend on what one *is*. This, first of all, must be focused on for the other two to be realized fully. This approach is based on Sidney Jourard's "*Integrity Therapy*," Carl Rogers' "*Client-Centered Therapy*," Thomas Gordon's "*P.E.T.*," and "*Gestalt*."

The counselors who emphasize right doing are impatient with the long process involved in the other therapies with little observable behavioral change. We do not have to go through all that intense self-examination; doing is possible without it and doing often leads to knowing and new being. The *Reality*

Therapy of William Glasser, *Behavioral Modification* and *Learning Theory* are some of the therapies of doing. *Assertiveness training* is also in this category. Oglesby considers all three styles to be an aid to the pastoral counselor and believes that biblical examples can be used in support of all three. He feels, however, that the therapy of being is most consistent with the biblical concept of persons. We do not wish to quarrel with this conclusion, nor do we wish to assume that one of the three styles of therapy has more validity than the others. To do so would be like arguing the old chicken or egg debate. We believe that knowing, doing, and being are important foci in understanding persons and that any change in one will bring about a change in the other two. We do wish to argue against suggestions that doing therapies necessarily are in violation of being or knowing therapies which have dominated pastoral counseling.

ASSERTION: A DOING THERAPY

The Bible always expresses faith in terms of obedience. "Not everyone who says to me, Lord, Lord, shall enter the kingdom of heaven, but he who does the will of my Father who is in heaven" (Matthew 7:21). Doing is essential to the believer; "Faith by itself, if it has no works is dead" (James 2:17). "Let us not love in word or speech but in deed and truth" (I John 3:18). The law of the Old Testament and the Kingdom of God as taught by Jesus stresses obedience.

The biblical narratives are rich examples for our own living. Modeling of right doing is very much a part of the teaching process of the Bible. The lives of its characters are valuable examples for the good life as well as for the tragic one. The Bible reveals a therapeutic approach that is very directive. "Be not anxious about your life" (Matthew 6:25). "Love your enemies, pray for

those who persecute you" (Matthew 5:44). "Love your
enemies and do good to those who hate you" (Luke
6:27). "Give to everyone who begs from you" (Luke
6:30). "As you wish men would do to you, do so to
them" (Luke 6:31). "If you lend to those from whom
you hope to receive, what credit is that to you?" (Luke
6:34) "Judge not and you will not be judged . . . forgive,
and you will be forgiven" (Luke 6:37). "Let every man
be quick to hear, slow to speak, slow to anger" (James
1:19). "Where jealousy and selfish ambition exist, there
will be disorder" (James 3:16). "We should love one
another" (I John 3:11). "And by this we knew him if we
keep his commandments" (I John 2:3).

Scripture does not hesitate to correct the believer
when he or she is wrong. "Temptations to sin are sure
to come; but woe to him by whom they come! . . . Take
heed to yourselves, if your brother sins rebuke him"
(Luke 17:1f). Just as the Apostle Paul rebuked Christians
in the church at Corinth:

> When you meet together, it is not the Lord's
> supper that you eat. For in eating, each one goes
> ahead with his own meal, and one is hungry and
> another is drunk. What! Do you not have a house
> to eat and drink in? Or do you despise the church
> of God and humiliate those who have nothing?
> What shall I say to you? Shall I commend you in
> this? No I will not (I Corinthians 11:20f).

The criticism of directive styles of therapy is not a
criticism of approach as much as of the direction itself.
Only the content of what is being taught can be called
into question by pastoral counselors not the fact that
teaching or directing is taking place. If directive therapy
is consistent with the content of Christian theology and
anthropology, then it should provide no difficulty.

Edward McAllister argues that the primary reason

assertiveness training is so useful to the Christian
therapist is that it provides better control. It is not only
an effective therapy but also an advocate of proper
expressions of emotion, which are modeled, rehearsed,
and commended from within the Christian context.[3]

The real burden of proof as to theological congruity
must be provided by the non-directive approaches to
therapy. There is nothing non-directive about the
religious characters in the Bible. The directive approach
is the apparent approach to relationships such as healing
and teaching.

The case has been well made for the non-directive
approach by a number of pastoral counselors but not at
the expense of directive approaches. Thomas Oden
recognizes that the Christian faith is basically
kerygmatic (preaching-oriented), while counseling should
not be preaching. Through a brilliant discussion of the
analogy of faith (*analogia fedei*) he shows that the Word
of God is experienced not only in proclamation but also
in relationships, which leaves the counseling relationship
as an important arena for God's self-disclosure. The
response to the Word is seen in our experience with
others. Rogers' non-directive, client-centered approach
is, in Oden's opinion, the most favorable counseling
style for this to happen.[4]

We support Oden's conclusions as to the value of
non-directive approaches in pastoral counseling but suggest
that his argument is supportive of both directive and non-
directive relationships. The response to the Word is
perceived in accepting relationships between patient and
counselee as well as in modeling, directing ones.

One gets the feeling from Oden that he perceives
any directive approaches or modeling as preaching.
Oden insists that counseling is not proclamation, and if
it seeks to impose upon the individual an answer that is
not his own, it loses its effectiveness. Thus it becomes
merely moralizing rather than true counseling.

While assertiveness therapy in its modeling, role-playing technique does run the risk of giving answers that are not the client's, it does so unintentionally. The assertive person must know his or her own self to choose consciously what behavior or part of the self is to be acted on. The role of the counselor is not to make that decision but to help the counselee practice doing and being what he or she chooses.

Pastoral counselors have a valid quarrel with behavioral therapists when they do make decisions for the counselee. Certainly B. F. Skinner's denial of freedom and dignity, suggesting that in operant conditioning the counselor manipulate the S^ds (discriminative stimuli) to program change, is in conflict with the Christian view. Skinner is critical of the Judeo-Christian perspective expressed by Hamlet's "How like a god!" and feels that Pavlov's formula "How like a dog!" is a step forward.[5]

Skinner is not at all concerned with what is inside the self. The inner self is only a reflection of the outer. He believes that just as physicists got nowhere by looking at the inside of falling objects, neither can psychology get anywhere by looking at states of mind, feelings, intentions.[6] Only the outward behavior of one in relation to environment is important for therapy.

Unfortunately, assertiveness trainers Fensterheim and Baer take this position too. They are interested in *doing* but neglect the questions of *being* and *knowing*. The result is a very unsatisfying analysis of the self. Unlike Skinner, they advocate *freedom* and *will power*. Assertive behavior is "up to you," they say. But then, siding with Skinner's analysis, which takes an entirely mechanistic environmental conditioning approach to human behavior, they conclude that if we do not like ourselves, we should not blame ourselves.[7] We should consider our choices habits, as though these were something outside the self. Nothing is up to us if we follow this line of thinking.

We would suggest that assertive, non-assertive, and aggressive behaviors are up to us. Our good choices, the ones we like as well as the ones we do not like, are a result of our will power, used either effectively or ineffectively.

Assertiveness training aids in practicing the effective exercise of our will power. When it deals only with the outward dimension of the self, however, without a look to the inner nature, it is hollow.

Two recent works show that assertiveness trainers are becoming directly involved with the inner nature. Michael Emmons' 1978 book, *The Inner Source*, is about getting in touch with the source inside.[8] This source has been given many names according to Emmons: the God-within, the Christ consciousness, the higher self, the superconscious. Keith Willcock, a psychologist from Canada, writing in the *Assert Newsletter* in August, 1979, indicates that in assertiveness one must develop a *knowingness* about the place within oneself from which assertive statements come.[9] He deals with this in terms of Assagioli's concept of the inner "self."

Jesus condemned legalism in his day because it viewed only the external action and practices of man and did not pay attention to the heart or inner motivation. The Christian perspective demands congruity between the inner and outer self, between being and doing. This happens through knowing. The three aspects of the self must be balanced.

The self is understood most fully when it is perceived in relation to God. Assertiveness therapy is best used in the Christian setting when one understands that the self, as given to us by God, needs expression. Lewis Sherrill once said that the self is made in relationships, and he intended this to also encompass the greater context of relationship with God.[10] Thomas Oden put this all in a syllogism, which rightly applies to all styles of therapy in the Christian setting:

(1)   *If genuine therapeutic growth is based upon human self-disclosure . . .*
(2)   *If authentic human self-disclosure exists as a response to divine revelation, as the kerygma suggests, then,*
(3)   *The divine self-disclosure is properly the precondition of authentic psychotherapeutic growth.*[11]

We know ourselves not by living as "persons alone," but by living in relationships. We know ourselves by coming to know others and expressing ourselves in these relationships. We know ourselves by coming to know and disclosing ourselves to God.

Assertive behavior is active self-disclosure. It is working at overcoming inhibitions for the expression of freedom. It is doing things that we truly wish to do. It is behavior congruent with our inner feelings. Assertiveness training provides clear ways of enhancing our relationships with others—providing us with greater opportunity for self-disclosure, self-knowledge, and God-knowledge.

If one can reach a total goal by knowing, being, and doing, then each individual will reach that goal by differing emphases. For some, knowing will be the focus, for some, being, and for others, doing. One will never take precedence over the others. We are reminded of the three *Margas* recommended by the Bhagavad Gita as paths to salvation: *Jnana Marga* (knowing), *Bhakti Marga* (loving), *Karma Marga* (doing or works); one may take a single path or several paths. Pastoral counselors might do well to heed the wisdom of Mohandus Gandhi, who recognized that we might favor one path over another but that no path is exclusive of the others.

In evaluating the three modes, knowing, being, and doing, we ought to recognize that each one can promote its counterpart. Knowing, for instance, is not always reached by passive methods. It may be and usually is enhanced by doing. Knowing also can prompt action. A therapy oriented toward the total person needs to use all three styles to promote health and growth.

That knowing is promoted by doing is the theme of the book of James. Knowing and not doing is "deceiving oneself." "For if anyone is a hearer of the Word and not a doer, he is like a man who observes his face in a mirror; for he observes himself and goes away and at once forgets what he was like" (James 1:23-24).

Assertiveness therapy is a valuable tool for the pastoral counselor in that it reinforces who we are through doing. It makes knowledge practical by application in life. It is most important to the pastoral counselor because his theology understands the call of Jesus in terms of obedience to God. "Not everyone who says to me, Lord, Lord, shall enter the kingdom of heaven, but he who does the will of my Father who is in heaven" (Matthew 7:21).

NOTES CHAPTER XII

1   Whereas the list could be quite long, we suggest several standards in the field of pastoral counseling: Paul Johnson, *Person and Counselor* (Nashville: Abingdon Press, 1967); Albert Outler, *Psychology and the Christian Message* (New York: Harper & Row, 1954); David Roberts, *Psychotherapy and the Christian View of Man* (New York: Charles Scribner's Sons, 1950); Thomas Oden, *Kerygma and Counseling* (Philadelphia: Westminster Press, 1966); Carroll Wise, *Pastoral Counseling: Its Theory and Practice* (New York: Harper & Row, 1951).

2   William B. Oglesby, "Pastoral Care and Counseling in Biblical Perspective," *Interpretation*, 27, July 1973.

3   Edward McAllister, "Assertion Training and the Christian Therapist," *Journal of Psychology and Theology*, Winter, 1975.

4   Oden, loc. cit.

5   B.F. Skinner, *Beyond Freedom and Dignity* (New York: Alfred Knopf, 1972), p. 201.

6   Ibid., p. 15. Note: Physicists have not concentrated solely on the external relationship of things. In his later years, Whitehead became very interested in the internal relationships of actual entities. His *Process and Reality* represents a great advancement not only for the metaphysics of his own field of math and physics but also for philosophy.

7   Herbert Fensterheim and Jean Baer, *Don't Say Yes When You Want to Say No* (New York: Dell Publishing Co., Inc., 1975) p. 183*ff*.

8   Michael L. Emmons, *The Inner Source* (San Luis Obispo, Calif.: Impact Publishers, Inc., 1978).

9   Keith Willcock, "The Assertive Self," *Assert 27*, (San Luis Obispo, Calif.: Impact Publishers, Inc. 1979).

10 Lewis Sherrill, *The Gift of Power* (New York: The MacMillan Co., 1963).

11 Oden, op. cit., p. 43.

APPENDIX I

ASSERTIVE TRAINING AND THE CHRISTIAN THERAPIST

by
Edward W. C. McAllister
Russell Sage College

Assertive training discussed by Wolpe (1973) and others gives the Christian therapist a useful tool to use in helping his clients achieve proper emotional expression. The techniques can be easily synthesized into the practice of the Christian therapist and allow the client to grow, relieve anxiety, and function meaningfully in interpersonal contacts and relationships.

The Christian therapist faces the unique position of having to define treatment strategies that are in harmony with the teachings of Jesus Christ and modern therapeutic thinking. The therapist must simultaneously be true to God and his profession. In establishing such a position, the therapist is best able to serve his clients and himself. The client ought to fully know that the Christian therapist is operating within the structure of Christianity, is using techniques that are designed to help the client with his problems and more fully help him understand the reality of the Christian perspective revealed by the "God who is there" through the Bible.

One technique that can be very useful to the Christian therapist, if used within the defined structure of Christianity, is assertive training. Wolpe (1973) states that:

> Assertive training is pre-eminently applicable to the deconditioning of unadaptive anxiety habits of response to people with whom the patient interacts. It makes use of the anxiety-inhibiting emotions that life situations evoke in him. A great many emotions, mostly pleasant in character, seem to invoke bodily events competitive with anxiety (Wolpe, 1958, p. 99). All categories of stimuli— sights, sounds, smells, words—may be sources of such emotions because of previous conditioning.
>
> A perfume, for example, may be conditioned to strong romantic feelings. In like fashion, another person may arouse approval, affection, admiration, annoyance, or anger or other feelings, each of which produce bodily responses different from anxiety and possibly competitive with it. It seems that when such emotions are exteriorized in motor behavior their intensity is enhanced; and any anxiety that is evoked by the situation is more likely to be inhibited.
>
> Assertive behavior is defined as the proper expression of any emotion other than anxiety towards another person (pp. 80-81).

Rimm and Masters (1974) point out that assertive behavior is "honest" and relatively "straight forward" behaviors that involve actual emotional states. Lazarus (1971) states:

> Wolpe proposed the term assertiveness in place of excitation, but many people associate 'assertive training' with one-upmanship and other deceptive games and plays which Wolpe includes under this heading and which have no place in the forthright and honest expression of one's basic feelings. Besides the word assertive cannot (unless stretched beyond its lexical boundaries) convey all the nuances of 'emotional freedom' which would include the subtleties of love and affection, empathy and compassion, admiration and appreciation, curiosity and interest, as well as anger, pain, remorse, skepticism, fear, and sadness. Training in emotional freedom implies the recognition and appropriate expression of each and every affective state (p. 116).

There are many people who do not know how to express either positive or negative feelings in their behavior. They either censor behaviors reflecting negative or positive feelings or allow their emotional state to release behaviors that are considered to be inappropriate by others and/or themselves. Such situations may cause a good deal of interpersonal or intrapersonal conflict.

Rimm and Masters (1974) define assertive training as follows:

> Simply stated, assertive training includes any therapeutic procedure aimed at increasing the client's ability to engage in such behavior in a socially appropriate manner. Behavioral goals

usually include the expression of negative feelings such as anger and resentment, but often assertive procedures are employed to facilitate the expression of positive feelings such as affection and praise (p. 81).

Many Christians are in need of assertive training because they view being non-assertive as part of their Christianity. This may be particularly true of women. (Other Christians may be non-assertive simply because of a history of interpersonal problems.) However, such a view can be harmful as well as mistaken and can lead to problems as the individual is not able to avoid the covert anxiety, anger, and frustration that such a position determines. In addition, such a person may not be able to present an adequate witness for Jesus Christ if he is too threatened. Christianity very clearly teaches that the Christian should show in action such things as love, joy, peace, kindness, and goodness as produced by the Holy Spirit. An appropriate amount of assertiveness is required to express these emotions. Too many Christian men do not clearly and openly express positive emotions toward their wives, children, and friends. Somehow our culture has conditioned suppression of such emotional expressions. In addition, Christianity sets forth required structure for life and guidelines for discipline in the church. Persons of non-assertive nature often have difficulty in dealing with these Christian mandates.

Assertive training is also useful for the treatment of the overly aggressive (Rimm and Masters, 1974). There are many who show inappropriate, aggressive behavior physically and verbally. For many, even their Christian witness takes this format. Many children are constantly involved in verbal aggression in the home or school as well as the more serious problems of physical aggression. All of the above examples are instances where inappropriate behavior is set off under particular stimulus conditions. Therefore, going back to the definition, assertive training is in order where the therapist desires to help the client learn the proper expression of emotion toward another person. The goal is not unlike Christianity itself where through salvation and sanctification, man restores his relationship with God and man. It is often forgotten that fallen man is not only separated from God but also from his fellow man. As Christianity restores man to God, man becomes substantially healed. A Christian ought to be able to relate to his fellow man in full guidance of the Holy Spirit. In so doing, man will express appropriate behavior. For many people, training is required to overcome habits, fears, and anxieties that exist in the area of interpersonal behavior. Locke (1971) quotes Wolpe's own description of the effects of self-assertion:

> Most assertive trainees seem to follow a similar pattern of evolution. First, there is an increased awareness of their non-assertiveness and its negative repercussions. This is followed by an intellectual appreciation of assertive behavior and its positive effects. Increasing distaste for their own ineffectuality and resentment toward the forces which seem to be maintaining or reinforcing the non-assertiveness soon lead to tentative, usually clumsy, attempts at self-assertive responses.
>
> If positive effects ensue, the probability of engaging in more assertive behavior increases. Occasionally, as emotional satisfactions intensify and spread, previously timid and dominated individuals tend to overassert themselves . . . (eventually) . . . the patient learns to be dominant without being dominating. . . . Finally, as the patient becomes aware of his growing mastery of interpersonal situations, there develops a genuine

and fitting indifference to minor slights, petty machinations, small irrationalities, and other insignificant 'pinpricks' of daily interaction . . . an additional consequence of assertive training is a changed self-concept. More adequate behavior elicits positive feedback from other individuals, and this may modify existing negative self-perceptions in a way that facilitates the performance of the new behavior (p. 322).

Wolpe (1973) states that in 1949 Salter proposed six modes of behavior for assertive training:

(1) *Feeling Talk*—By this Salter means the deliberate use of spontaneously felt emotions. An example he gives is, 'Thank heavens, today is Friday and the weekend is here,' in contrast to saying dryly, 'Today is Friday.'

(2) *Facial Talk*—This is the display of emotion in face and movement as far as it is appropriate.

(3) *Contradict and Attack*—When the patient disagrees with someone he is not to pretend agreement, but to contradict with as much feeling as is reasonable.

(4) *The Use of I*—The word 'I' is used as much as possible so as to involve the patient in the statements he makes.

(5) *Express Agreement When You Are Praised*—Praise should not be warded off, but accepted honestly. Self-praise should also be volunteered when reasonable.

(6) *Improvise*—Try to make spontaneous responses to immediate stimuli.

It should again be noted lest the reader react inappropriately, that assertive behaviors are the "proper expressions of emotion." The Christian therapist's

structure is going to control this domain. The therapist
will be giving feedback to the client during the therapy
sessions so that the client will receive information about
how his attempts at assertive behavior will be received.
    How is the need for assertive training determined?
Rimm and Masters (1974) state that patients rarely ask
for this specific treatment. Normally, the therapist
makes the assessment of the client's needs through the
behavior therapy interview. In addition, there are
inventories such as the Wolpe-Lazarus Assertive
Inventory (Wolpe-Lazarus, 1966), the Rathus Assertive
Schedule (Rathus, 1974), and the Assertive
Questionnaire (Lazarus, 1971). In essence, the client
clearly shows interpersonal problems and reports anxiety
or fear in specified social situations.
    It is necessary to explain the technique of assertive
training to the client initially. Rimm and Masters (1974,
pp. 87-91) make the following points in this regard:
    (1) Persons who have considerable difficulty
         expressing (emotions) often believe not only that
         it is wrong to express (emotions) overtly, but
         that it is equally wrong (for example) to 'think
         angry thoughts.'
    (2) We recommend that feelings of trust and
         confidence be first established and that the
         subject of the client's hostile feelings be dealt
         with in a graduated fashion.
    (3) It is likely that for many clients in need of
         assertive training, significant prior attempts at
         assertion were met with highly unpleasant
         consequences. While it is usually true that the
         client cannot be expected to know this, it is the
         therapist's task to point this out within the
         specific context of the client's current
         difficulties.
    It must be pointed out to the client that much of
the worry, fear, or anxiety that he experiences in

interpersonal situations is irrational and represents inappropriate behavioral exchange. One procedure that may be followed with the Christian client is to show the client incidences of assertive behavior in the Bible. Through this procedure the client, who may have initial problems with the concept of assertive training, can be shown that there is not a violation of Christian teachings in assertive training, but rather the goal is to achieve proper, reasoned responses congruent with real Christianity. Below are some of the assertive categories selected from the book of Mark (*Good News for Modern Man*).

(1) *Feeling Talk*—Mark 3:1-6. Then Jesus went back to the synagogue, where there was a man who had a crippled hand. Some people were there who wanted to accuse Jesus of doing wrong; so they watched him closely to see whether he would cure anyone on the Sabbath. Jesus said to the man with the crippled hand, 'Come up here to the front.' Then he asked the people: 'What does our Law allow us to do on the Sabbath? To help or to harm? To save a man's life or destroy it?' But they did not say a thing. Jesus was angry as he looked around at them, but at the same time he felt sorry for them, because they were so stubborn and wrong. Then he said to the man, 'Stretch out your hand.' He stretched it out and it became well again. So the Pharisees left the meeting house and met at once with some members of Herod's party; and they made plans against Jesus to kill him.

Mark 9:17-19. A man in the crowd answered: 'Teacher, I brought my son to you, because he has an evil spirit in him and cannot talk. Whenever the spirit attacks him, it throws him on the ground and he foams at the mouth, grits his teeth, and becomes stiff all over. I asked your disciples to drive the

spirit out, but they could not.' Jesus said to them:
'How unbelieving you people are! How long must I
stay with you? How long do I have to put up with
you? Bring the boy to me.'

Mark 10:13-15. Some people brought children
to Jesus for him to touch them, but the disciples
scolded the people. When Jesus noticed it, he was
angry and said to the disciples: 'Let the children
come to me! Do not stop them, because the
Kingdom of God belongs to such as these.
Remember this! Whoever does not receive the
Kingdom of God like a child will never enter it.'

(2) *Facial Talk*—Mark 10:20-22. 'Teacher,' the
man said, 'ever since I was young I have obeyed all
these commandments.' With love Jesus looked
straight at him and said: 'You need only one thing.
Go and sell all that you have and give the money
to the poor, and you will have riches in heaven;
then come and follow me.' When the man heard
this, gloom spread over his face and he went away
sad, because he was very rich.

(3) *Contradict and Attack*—Mark 2:23-27. Jesus
was walking through some wheat fields on a
Sabbath day. As his disciples walked along with
him, they began to pick the heads of wheat. So the
Pharisees said to Jesus, 'Look, it is against our Law
for your disciples to do this on the Sabbath.' Jesus
answered: 'Have you never read what David did
that time when he needed something to eat? He
and his men were hungry, so he went into the
house of God and ate the bread offered to God.
This happened when Abiathar was the High Priest.
According to our Law only the priests may eat of
this bread—but David ate it, and even gave it to his
men.' And Jesus said, 'The Sabbath was made for
the good of man; man was not made for the
Sabbath.'

(4) *The Use of I*—Mark 3:13-15. Then Jesus went up a hill and called to himself the men he wanted. They came to him and he chose twelve, whom he named apostles. 'I have chosen you to stay with me,' he told them; 'I will also send you out to preach, and you will have authority to drive out demons.'

Mark 14:60-62. The High Priest stood up in front of them all and questioned Jesus: 'Have you no answer to the accusation they bring against you?' But Jesus kept quiet and would not say a word. Again the High Priest questioned him: 'Are you the Messiah, the Son of the Blessed God?' 'I am,' answered Jesus, 'and you will all see the Son of Man seated at the right side of the Almighty and coming with the clouds of heaven!'

(5) *Express Agreement When You Are Praised*—Mark 8:27-30. Then Jesus and his disciples went away to the villages of Caesarea Philippi. On the way he asked them, 'Tell me, who do people say that I am?' 'Some say that you are John the Baptist,' they answered; 'others say that you are Elijah, while others say that you are one of the prophets.' 'What about you?' he asked them. 'Who do you say I am?' Peter answered, 'You are the Messiah.' Then Jesus ordered them, 'Do not tell anyone about me.'

(6) *Improvise*—Mark 12:13-17. Some Pharisees and some members of Herod's party were sent to Jesus to trap him with questions. They came to him and said, 'Teacher, we know that you are an honest man. You don't worry about what people think, because you pay no attention to what a man seems to be, but you teach the truth about God's will for man. Tell us, is it against our Law to pay taxes to the Roman Emperor? Should we pay them, or not?' But Jesus saw through their trick

and answered, 'Why are you trying to trap me?
Bring a silver coin and let me see it.' They brought
him one and he asked, 'Whose face and name are
these?' 'The Emperor's,' they answered. So Jesus
said, 'Well, then, pay to the Emperor what belongs
to him, and pay to God what belongs to God.'
And they were filled with wonder at him.

The above examples have been selected from Mark.
The same could be done with the book of Acts, the
writing of Paul, or other parts of the Bible.

The most common method of assertive training is
behavior rehearsal. Through this method the therapist
guides the client to express proper emotional expression
in the situations that are giving the client problems. The
therapist gives the client immediate feedback during
these role playing sessions. The therapist may also use
role reversal techniques during the behavior rehearsal
and the therapist may act as a model to the client. It is
within these two specific techniques in behavior
rehearsal—immediate feedback about the client's
behavior and modeling for the client—that the therapist
can insure that the training takes place within the
Christian structures of behavior.

A step that would be taken early in assertive
training would be to emphasize what Wolpe (1973) calls
commendatory assertive training. In this training the
client rehearses with the therapist verbal statements that
are appropriate in interpersonal contacts that the client
has from day to day. These verbal statements should
insure positive feedback outside of the therapist's office
and will develop the confidence of the client in assertive
training. It must be emphasized to the client, however,
that these statements are only to be used when
appropriate. That is, the client must recognize the
appropriate situation and genuinely feel that the verbal
statement is proper. Examples provided by Wolpe (1973)
are:

(1)   That is a beautiful dress/brooch, etc.
(2)   You look lovely, terrific, ravishing, glamorous, etc.
(3)   That was a clever remark.
(4)   What a radiant smile!
(5)   I like you.
(6)   I love you.
(7)   I admire your tenacity.
(8)   That was brilliantly worked out.

The therapist can easily provide additional comments appropriate for the particular client for behavior rehearsal. As the client uses these statements and grows in confidence he can then move to the proper expression of other emotions rather rapidly. These other trainings would show the client the proper and reasonable ways of expressing anger and frustration. Under the direction of the Christian therapist the expression of these emotions can be rehearsed and then used in the spirit of love that Francis Schaeffer (1973) has pointed out must be the "distinctive mark of the Christian."

McFall and Lillesand (1971) point out that behavior rehearsal has been described as one of the more promising of the available behavior modification approaches. McFall and Marston (1970) quote from Lazarus (1966) where it is reported that behavior rehearsal was effective in 86 percent of its cases in training patients to be more assertive. Direct advice therapies were successful in 44 percent of their cases, and non-directive therapies were successful in 32 percent of their cases. McFall and Marston (1970) found that automated and standardized response rehearsal treatments were effective in improving assertive performance.

McFall and Lillesand (1971) report that overt and covert behavior rehearsal are equally effective. Kazdin (1974) reports results that support the use of assertive training using models and models with reinforcement.

In short, the assertive training procedures used can
vary a great deal. The therapist may use models or not,
may allow the client to rehearse directly and may apply
feedback, may use covert rehearsal with imagery, and a
number of other kinds of specific modeling procedures.
What does seem clear is that the treatment of the client
should be specific. The client should rehearse behaviors
that involve the specific problems that the client is
experiencing. Although there may be some
generalization of effect, maximal benefit seems to accrue
with specific trainings. Rimm and Masters (1974)
summarize the technique as follows:

(1) The client enacts the behavior as he would in
    real life.
(2) The therapist provides specific verbal feedback
    stressing positive features, and presenting
    inadequacies in a friendly, non-punitive fashion.
(3) The therapist models more desirable behavior,
    with the client assuming the other person's role
    when appropriate.
(4) The client then attempts the response again.
(5) The therapist bountifully rewards improvement.
    If necessary, steps (3) and (4) are repeated until
    both therapist and client are satisfied with the
    response and the client can engage in the
    response with little or no anxiety.
(6) The interaction, if it is at all lengthy, should be
    broken up into small segments, dealt with
    sequentially. Following this, the client and
    therapist may wish to run through the entire
    interaction for the purpose of consolidating
    gains.
(7) In an interchange involving the expression of
    negative feelings, the client should be instructed
    to begin with a relatively mild response.
    However, he should also be given responses in
    case the initial response is ineffective.

(8) In rehearsing the expression of negative feelings, objective statements pertaining to annoying or hurtful behaviors on the part of the other person are far superior to personal attacks, which are often irrelevant and have the effect of backing the other into a corner.

Finally, is assertive training better than other techniques for Christians? A clear answer is not really possible since no research data is available. However, research mentioned above has indicated that assertive training has been useful for clients. The Christian therapist can use this technique to help the Christian client better fit his life experiences and Christianity. In order for the Holy Spirit to freely act, the Spirit-filled Christian must respond as he is led. In addition, Christianity sets forth guidelines for life that are not always easy to follow. The Christian in today's society should show proper emotional response in the context of Christianity. The Christian therapist may use assertive training to help accomplish this.

BIBLIOGRAPHY APPENDIX I

Kazdin, A. E. "Effects of Covert Modeling and Models Reinforcement on Assertive Training," *Journal of Abnormal Psychology*, 1974, 83, 240-252.

Lazarus, A. A. *Behavior Therapy and Beyond*. New York: McGraw-Hill, 1971.

Locke, E. A. "Is Behavior Therapy Behavioristic? An Analysis of Wolpe's Psycho Therapeutic Methods," *Psychological Bulletin*, 1971, 76, 318-327.

McFall, R. M. and Marston, A. R. "An Experimental Investigation of Behavior Rehearsal in Assertive Training," *Journal of Abnormal Psychology*, 1970, 76, 295-303.

McFall, R. M. and Lillesand, D. B. "Behavior Rehearsal With Modeling and Coaching in Assertive Training," *Journal of Abnormal Psychology*, 1971, 77, 313-325.

Rathus, S. A. "A Thirty Item Schedule for Assessing Assertive Behavior," in E. J. Thomas (eds.), *Behavior Modification Procedure—A Sourcebook*. Chicago: Aldine, 1974.

Rimm, D. C. and Masters, J. C. *Behavior Therapy: Techniques and Empirical Findings*. New York: Academic Press, 1974.

Schaeffer, F. A. *The Mark of the Christian*. Downers Grove, Illinois: InterVarsity Press, 1970.

Wolpe, J. E. *The Practice of Behavior Therapy*. New York: Pergamon Press, 1973.

Appendix I quoted in its entirety from *Journal of Psychology and Theology*, Winter, 1975.

APPENDIX II

BOOKS ON ASSERTIVENESS

Adler, R.B. *Confidence in Communication: A Guide to Assertive and Social Skills.* New York: Holt, Rinehart & Winston, 1974.

Alberti, R.E. and M.L. Emmons. *Your Perfect Right: A Guide to Assertive Behavior.* San Luis Obispo, Calif.: Impact Publishers, Inc., 1970, 2nd edition, 1974, 3rd edition, 1978.

Alberti, R.E., ed. *Assertiveness: Innovations, Applications, Issues.* San Luis Obispo, Calif.: Impact Publishers, Inc. 1977.

Alberti, R.E. and M.L. Emmons. *Stand Up, Speak Out, Talk Back!* New York: Pocket Books (Simon & Schuster), 1975.

Augsburger, D. *Anger and Assertiveness in Pastoral Care.* Philadelphia: Fortress Press, 1979.

Baer, J. *How to Be an Assertive (Not Aggressive) Woman in Life, in Love, and on the Job.* New York: Signet (New American Library), 1976.

Bloom, L.Z., K. Coburn and J. Pearlman. *The New Assertive Woman.* New York: Delacorte Press, 1975.

Bower, S.A. and G.H. Bower. *Asserting Yourself.* Reading, Mass.: Addison-Wesley, 1976.

Butler, P. *Self-Assertion for Women: A Guide to Becoming Androgynous.* San Francisco: Canfield Press, 1976.

Cheek, D.K. *Assertive Black . . . Puzzled White.* San Luis Obispo, Calif.: Impact Publishers, Inc., 1976.

Chenevert, M. *Special Techniques for Women in the Health Professions.* St. Louis: Mosby, 1978.

Clark, C.C. *Assertive Skills for Nurses.* Wakefield, Mass.: Contemporary Publishing Co., 1978.

Cotler, S.B. and J.J. Guerra. *Assertion Training.* Champaign, Ill.: Research Press, 1976.

Fensterheim, H. and J. Baer. *Don't Say Yes When You Want to Say No.* New York: David McKay, 1975.

Galassi, M.D. and J.P. Galassi. *Assert Yourself: An Assertion Training Workbook.* New York: Human Sciences Press, 1976.

Gambrill, E.D. and C.A. Richey. *It's Up to You: The Development of Assertive Social Skills.* Millbrae, Calif.: Les Femmes, 1976.

Hauck, P.A. *How to Stand Up for Yourself.* Philadelphia: Westminster Press, 1979.

Herman, S.J. *Becoming Assertive: A Guide for Nurses.*
New York: D. VanNostrand Co., 1978.

Jakubowski, P. and A.J. Lange. *The Assertive Option.*
Champaign, Ill.: Research Press, 1978.

Kelley, C. *Assertion Training: A Facilitator's Guide.* La
Jolla, Calif.: University Associates, 1979.

Kelley, J.D. and B.J. Winship. *Assertive Training.*
Chicago: Nelson-Hall, 1976.

Lange, A.J. and P. Jakubowski. *Responsible Assertive
Behavior.* Champaign, Ill.: Research Press, 1976.

Lazarus, A.A. and A. Fay. *I Can If I Want To.* New
York: William Morrow, 1975.

Liberman, R.P., et al. *Personal Effectiveness.* Champaign,
Ill.: Research Press, 1976.

Markel, G. *Parents Are to Be Seen and Heard:
Assertiveness in Educational Planning for Handicapped
Children.* San Luis Obispo, Calif.: Impact
Publishers, Inc., 1979.

Osborn, S.M. and G.G. Harris. *Assertive Training for
Women.* Springfield, Ill.: Charles C. Thomas, 1975.

Palmer, P. *The Mouse, the Monster and Me.* San Luis
Obispo, Calif.: Impact Publishers, Inc., 1977.

Palmer, P. *Liking Myself.* San Luis Obispo, Calif.: Impact
Publishers, Inc., 1977.

Paris, C. and B. Casey. *Project You: A Manual of
Rational Assertiveness Training.* Denver: Institute of
Skills Education, 1979.

Phelps, S. and N. Austin. *The Assertive Woman*. San Luis Obispo, Calif.: Impact Publishers, Inc., 1975.

Salter, A. *Conditioned Reflex Therapy*. New York: Farrar, Straus, and Giroux, 1949 (Capricorn Books edition, 1961).

Seattle-King County N.O.W. *Woman, Assert Yourself!* New York: Harper & Row, 1974.

Shaw, M.E. *Assertive-Responsive Management: A Personal Handbook*. Reading, Mass.: Addison-Wesley, 1979.

Smith, M.J. *When I Say No, I Feel Guilty*. New York: Dial Press, 1975.

Taetzsch, L. and E. Benson. *Taking Charge: On the Job Techniques for Assertive Management*. Chicago: Nelson-Hall, 1978.

Taubman, B. *How to Become an Assertive Woman*. New York: Pocket Books (Simon & Schuster), 1976.